Everything is Coming up Roses
in this Beautiful Book

BOUQUET OF
LOVE AND PASSION

Belongs to: _Kathie Hulquist_
1-2-23
Monday

Simple & Creative Ways
to Nurture Heaven's Beauty

Love, Joy, & Peace

ENJOY ROSES EVERY DAY

Volume 1

How to Romance "The Rose" with Passion Outside

Outside in Your Garden with Passion
Each and Every Day for the
"Master Gardener" — Our Abba Father God

author & artist
SUSAN PETTIT

Copyright © 2022 by Susan Pettit
Enjoy Roses Every Day: How to Romance "The Rose" With Passion Outside
Written and illustrated by Susan Pettit
Printed in the United States of America.
ISBN: 978-1-68556-733-0
All rights reserved solely by the author. The author and artist guarantee all content is original and does not infringe upon the legal rights of any other person or work. No part of this book may be reproduced in any form without the permission of the author and artist. The views expressed in this book are not necessarily those of the publisher.
All Scripture quotations are from the New King James Version®, Copyright © 1982 by Thomas Nelson. Used by permission. All rights reserved.
Pre-press editors: Diana Richardson and Amanda Thompson
All artwork and photography by the author and artist Susan Pettit (www.SPettitGallery.com)
Author's back cover photo: Jeannette Klobetanz
Cover design by: Kelly Stewart

The author wishes to express gratitude to the Lord for His loving kindness and faithfulness. In response to His prompting, love, and inspiration, **100% of all profits of this book will go to support** my fellow workers, brothers and sisters in Christ, as they serve orphans and widows here in the USA, Kenya East Africa, the Ukraine, and around the world.
Thank you for investing in the Kingdom of God.
Shalom and May God Bless You Abundantly!

S. Pettit Gallery: www.SPettitGallery.com; spettitgallery@gmail.com
Heaven's Love Light: www.heavenslovelight.com; heavenslovelight@gmail.com

Kathie,
May the Lord fill you with more of His great love, joy, and peace!

Blessings,
Susan S. Pettit
Nehemiah 8:10

via Mo'in Mike

Day Breaker is a lovely rose, and in this photo it fills my heart with love seeing God's loving signature written in it.

DEDICATION

I dedicate the love of my heart
to my loving Heavenly Father,
The original and creative Master Gardener,
With all of my heart full of love and adoration.

Elohim,
My King, my God, and my Mighty Creator
Thank You, Elohim.
You are my Master Gardener,
The One Who created the rose,
As well as the vast Cosmos for all to see.

You Are My great and loving God,
Who crafted us out of clay, dirt, and dust,
Yet immortal, supernatural, and full of light,
For all of eternity.

Oh God, You created this world,
As You simply spoke, the Word stepped out,
Then Holy Spirit powerfully breathed life,
Into every element of this very good and beautiful world.

In the beginning God created the heavens and the earth.

— PHILIPPIANS 2:9–11

Fear not, for I am with you;
Be not dismayed, for I am your God.
I will strengthen you,
Yes, I will help you,
I will uphold you with My righteous right hand.

— ISAIAH 41:10

ACKNOWLEDGMENTS

"La Vie en Rose!"

ROMANTICALLY TRANSLATED:
TO SEE WITH ROSE COLORED GLASSES

This is for all the rose lovers and gardeners of the world—
You who see this amazingly designed terrestrial ball that
we call earth through rose-colored glasses and always
have the seed of faith and hope in your heart that the
Lord gives love and beauty with the promise of spring.

I wish to thank my dear family and friends for the many years of love, patience, kindness, prayers, sacrifice, and support you have given me as I have struggled along my journey to find and fulfill my calling and destiny. The following are some of the most fragrant bouquets God sent to help and cheer me along my pathway to heaven.

My children: Liz, Jessica, and Melody and grandson Wyatt; you are my biggest blessings and have been so supportive in my artistic journey. I love you all bunches and bunches beyond the stars forever.

My family: my parents, James and Phyllis Pettit, and my sister and her husband, Mary Ann and Dwaine; thank you for being the best parents, grandparents, sister, auntie, and uncle hand-picked by God as the cream of the crop for me and my children! Thank you for raising me in a God-fearing home and giving me love and elbow room to be creative and giving me a space in the garden and rose bed. Love you all so much.

My friends: Barb, Cherri, Clare, Della, Diana, Elaine, E. W., Fritzi, Gail, Geri, Janet, Jeanne, Kimberly, Lesley, Linda, Louise, Mark, Nancy, Neva, Norma, Paul, Rachel, Randal, Roseann, Susan, and Terry; you all have seen the good, the bad, and the ugly in my days and yet still love me for who I am. I am eternally grateful. The Lord carefully selected a beautiful bouquet of friends to help me grow and blossom through my journey in the garden. I love you and pray for you.

My mentor: Barbara Leachman. You have wisely advised, guided, pruned, and shaped me as I have passionately followed my dreams and life work for my Lord. You are amazing! Thank you from the bottom of my grateful, creative, entrepreneurial heart.

With a heart full of gratitude, love, and thanksgiving to our Lord Jesus for each of you, I thank you so much! I look forward to spending eternity with you. We shall spend light years of eternity with our beloved Father God, King Jesus, and Holy Spirit, they continue to grow our love for them and our roses for all time.

With love forever and always,

Susan Pettit

ARTISAN, GARDENER, & SCRIBE
FOR THE KING OF GLORY

Adorable Bentley, an Aussiedoodle, who is one of my priceless grand fur babies. He lives in Alaska with my daughter and son-in-law.

CONTENTS

INTRODUCTION 1

Volume 1: **OUTSIDE**
ENJOY GROWING YOUR ROSE BOUQUET EVERY DAY.... 7

Chapter 1
ROSES ARE THE BEST 9
    Roses are Queen... 11
    Thorns and Thrones...................................... 12
    Thorns in Heaven 12
    My Rose Love Story 14
    The Romance of the Rose 16
    Fragrance 18
    Rose Buds of Blessings 23

Chapter 2
SO MANY GORGEOUS ROSES
& NOT ENOUGH TIME OR SPACE 25
    Roses Galore... 27
    The Main Types of Roses 27
    What Makes a Wild Rose 29
    Old Garden Roses 30
    Modern Garden Roses 30
    Grafted vs Own-Root Roses........................ 35
    Grafted Roses 35
    Own-Root Roses 36
    Picture Books and Catalogs........................ 38
    Decisions, Decisions.................................... 39
    How to Select Your Beauty 40
    The Hunt Begins 44
    Rose Buds of Blessings 46

Chapter 3
COMPOSING YOUR VIBRANT ROSE CANVAS WITH COLOR & FRAGRANCE 49
- Seven Years Old 51
- Fourteen Years Old 53
- My First Rose.. 55
- Start with a Dream and a Vision for Your Canvas 57
- Understanding Roses 58
- Rose Buds of Blessings 62

Chapter 4
SECRETS FOR GROWING STUNNING ROSES TO TURN BOTH HEADS & NOSES 65
- The Crown Wears Thorns 67
- Not All Roses Are Created Equal......................... 70
- Susan's Steps for Simply *Scent-sational* Success with Roses..... 72
- Order Your Roses....................................... 72
- The Secret Recipe....................................... 73
- #1 Top Secret: Feed the Soil and the Soil Feeds the Rose..... 74
- #2 Top Secret: Prune to Keep Your Rose Clean 77
- #3 Top Secret: Love Your Rose 79
- Rose Buds of Blessings 82

Chapter 5
ENERGETIC ROSES LOVE ORGANIC MEALS & COMFY BLANKETS.................... 85
- From the Ground Up 87
- Tools for the Trade..................................... 87
- Warning 88
- Natural Ingredients..................................... 89
- Fish Story 90
- The Big Five 91
- Extra Ingredients for the Beauty and Strength of Your Roses . 92
- Dig Deep and Wide 94

    The Planting 94
    Plain and Simple Everyday Planting 100
    Mulching Is the Magic Carpet 103
    Mulch 104
    Mulching Trick 106
    Spring and Fall Feeding 107
    Hope 108
    Supernatural Hope 109
    Taking Care of the Bad Guys 112
    Aphid and Bad Bug Spray 112
    One More Secret 113
    Energy Drink 114
    Rose Energy Drink 115
    A Surprising Top Secret— Heavenly Help 116
    Prayer 120
    Rose Buds of Blessings 121

THIS IS NOT THE END 125
THE END NOTES FOR A NEW BEGINNING . . 127

RESOURCES 131
RECOMMENDED READING 132
ROSES 133
SUPPLIES 133

ABOUT THE AUTHOR AND ARTIST 137

INTRODUCTION

My beloved spoke, and said to me: "Rise up, my love, my fair one, and come away."

— SONG OF SOLOMON 2:10

What are you passionate about?
What makes your heart throb and your pulse race?
Are you a person of passion and a passionate lover?
Do you have a real and authentic love of life and all the beauty that is in it?

The answer for me is YES!

When I was a little girl, my nickname was "Suzy Sunshine." I was born to love color, fragrance, and light. I will forever be a lover of roses. I am in love with their hues, shades, splendor, perfume, and romance.

Many individuals refer to me as "The Rose Lady."

I am crazy in love with roses. I eat, sleep, drink, and wear roses, (Yes, *for real*).

My beautiful roses get much tender loving care from me. I tenderly cultivate and grow my lovely roses. At one crazy time I had more than two hundred rosebushes! God has blessed me to be able to pick and share their beauty and fragrance with others (they beg to be shared as they are just too wonderful to keep). I carefully arrange and happily give colorful roses away. But I also am passionate about drawing, sketching, and painting my lovely roses.

Yet, my elaborate and over-the-top zeal for the queen of flowers pales in comparison to my obsessive passion for "The Rose," Whose name means friend, Redeemer, and Savior— the Lord Jesus Christ, the Creator of my beloved roses and the Lover of our souls.

I love and adore the One True Rose, King Jesus, the Lamb of Glory, and the Lion of Judah. My heart beats passionately in love with Abba Father, and I look for Him everywhere. My soul sings in sync with precious Holy Spirit as He is all around me at all times. My passionate heart cannot get enough of Their beauty, Their light, each of the Trinity's love and fragrance.

This book is a heart work about roses and, I promise, you will learn how to grow, enjoy, and love gorgeous roses in abundance outside along with how to bring those beauties inside your home.

But much more importantly, as you read this three-volume romance, you will learn how to fall passionately and completely in love with the Creator of the rose— our Creator and our beloved Heavenly Father and Abba; the One True Rose, the Prince of Peace, our brother, our shepherd, and our Savior— King Jesus Christ; and the beloved Drama King of all of heaven— Holy Spirit, Who loves color, fragrance, pageantry, production, the arts, and of course drama both in heaven and on this beautiful planet, throughout the cosmos, and all of heaven.

King Jesus gave up heaven to bring His light into our darkness. He came down to earth so we would be able to leave earth and go up to live in heaven forever! The Perfect Rose of Calvary was cut off at the root. Our beautiful Lord Jesus Christ was brutally beaten and cruelly crowned with a wicked crown of thorns. He was nailed on a tree, naked and alone for all to see. He was bleeding and dying all alone for you and me. Though innocent, He was wrongfully accused yet willingly took the blame for you and me. He died a brutal sinner's death for all humanity.

The Royal Rose, the King of Glory, died hanging on the Cross over 2,000 years ago for you and me. Three days later, with the Holy Spirit's dunamis resurrection power, He arose up out of the earthen grave as our hope and glory forever and ever.

Currently, in our world, chaos is all around us with the aftermath of the novel corona virus (SARS-CoV-2 or Covid-19) and many other crises and war on many soils. There are still losses of all kinds in health, lives, families, jobs, finances, and other areas. There is constant pandemonium bombarding us. We are dealing with questions that seem unanswerable. Fear is all about us. We do not know where to turn or how to get through our lives in this worldwide chaos.

As I sit with my Lord Jesus in my tiny sun-drenched art studio and gallery with a cup of tea in hand and look out over my color-filled rose garden flitting with bees and butterflies, the peace of God descends into my little corner of the world. Ah, His comfort and hope; His love, joy, and peace are beyond words and price. Jesus meets me each day in the garden.

The Abba is calling you, my friend, into the garden for intimacy.

These are the things that the Abba told me to share with you, dear rose lover and reader. Your Papa God is calling you, my friend, into the garden for intimacy. We are in a new era. This is the time to be lured into the rose garden with the Lord to learn as we lean into Him.

We will learn together how to fall passionately in love with the Creator of your beautiful soul and walk with Him in the cool of the garden of your heart, just you and Him. You will be alone together and growing more and more in love with each other. A beautiful sight! And I am here to help you get there, my friend.

If you really love growing roses, then dig into Volume One right away and find out to how to grow the most dazzling roses on your block or in your area. Volume 2 focuses on how to get the most of your cut roses and best use them for bringing beauty and fragrance and joy into your home and life. In Volume 3, be on the lookout for delightful surprises along with some powerful truths to flame your passion of love in your heart and soul for "The Rose," King Jesus. It is my hope there is a little something to help each and every one to grow as I share my everyday passions with you.

Know that I have prayed for you as the Holy Spirit has guided me in writing. It is my hope and prayer, with expectation, that heaven will open up over you and the Father's great love will come pouring out in unprecedented ways upon you. My prayers with devotion are asking for the Lord's blessings to overtake you in His beauty, joy, and peace as He shatters the darkness with His love and light in and around you.

Before you wander on, I encourage you to read the following blessing out loud over both yourself and your loved ones:

> Dear Heavenly Father,
> I pray in the loving Name of our Jesus,
>
> *Help me to **Stop**—* and consider Your handiwork in the heavens as well as Your love in my heart and life.
>
> *Help me to **Look**—* and actually see Your glorious signature in every petal and my own unique fingerprints.
>
> *Help me to **Listen**—* to recognize Your majesty and glory in Your voice as You speak through all of creation.
>
> *Help me to **Rest**—* under Your shadow as the Almighty, at peace and together with You, in Your secret place.
>
> Please open the eyes and ears of my heart to receive Your wisdom, knowledge, and understanding in the revelation of Who You are, and that the eyes of my heart will be enlightened today with Your loving existence in all I am in You, and all You are in everything seen and not seen every day.
>
> In Jesus name, amen.

With love from a fellow ardent rose lover of the LORD, as one of the King's gardeners, artist, and scribe, sending love and blessings always,

Susan Pettit

Volume 1

OUTSIDE

**ENJOY GROWING YOUR
ROSE BOUQUET EVERY DAY**

*The signature of God
is written in Flowers!*

— HENRI MATISSE

Falling In Love has such a rich and heavenly fragrance! The heavy rose perfume makes it worth fighting for as you try to pick it with its countless wicked thorns. This marvelous cut rose can last up to ten days in a vase.

Chapter 1

ROSES ARE THE BEST

From the thorn bush comes forth the rose.

— JEWISH PROVERB

ROSES ARE QUEEN

*Roses are the Queen of Hearts
and they have stolen our hearts
with their beauty, fragrance, and love.*

Go ahead and say the word rose out loud. Instantly get an image in your mind's eye of some sort of beauty and your nose may even sense a whiff of sweet fragrance.

Plain and simple, roses represent many things to many people. Roses represent love and romance. Some feel they embody beauty, fragrance, hope, and joy. For others, roses symbolize gifts and celebration; yet others, life and death. What do they mean to you?

Roses are a universal symbol of beauty, love, and romance in any country and language. All through history, many have believed that roses are Queen of Flowers. There are songs, poems, art, and so much more that reflect the beauty and passion of a rose.

We love our roses. They are interwoven in our celebrations of love and joy and memories of milestones and sadness. Roses can be given by the dozens to commemorate the winner at a winner's circle, they can be given as a single rose to convey "I love you," and they can be placed carefully on a grave. They can be given simply to put a smile on someone's face to say, "I'm thinking of you."

THORNS AND THRONES

*It is not all roses
when it comes to roses.*

Roses are a part of our world history. Kings and wars have been named after the rose. In ancient history they were recorded through writing and in art. They have been given in celebrations and memorials. Songs have been sung about the rose. Others have fiercely fought to keep their legacy alive.

For millennia, roses have been known for their exquisite beauty, glorious color, romantic form, and magnificent fragrance. And the fascination for the rose— in all of its beauty— continues today.

THORNS IN HEAVEN

*He who wants the rose
must respect the thorn.*

— PERSIAN PROVERB

Roses are famous for their soft and voluptuous blossoms, but they have a bloody, dark, and dangerous side as well. You might even say, "It is not all roses when it comes to roses."

Yes, you guessed it. It is painful when a stinkin' thorn grabs your flesh and sinks in to draw red blood. Not all roses are created equal in their look and bloom, nor are they in their stem, strength, and deadly thorn.

It seems to me, that the more fragrant the rose, the more wicked their thorns. Have you noticed that too? It seems to me that the stronger the fragrance lures you in for a good sniff, the more those tenacious thorns fight you to keep its blossoms intact on the bush. And then you feel that familiar "ouch" and look down to see red drops of blood.

One of my favorite roses is Falling in Love, which is a beautiful, warm pink and soft ivory. If you could smell those roses (and, oh, how I wish you could), you would experience a smell of heaven in its glorious fragrance; it is the scent you would find captured and sold in a fine perfume. Beware! To pick a single rose from Falling in Love, you will question that love, as you may need to go out in full armor to carefully cut one perfect bud off the bush. It has the wickedest thorns ever! I have had to sport much lavender essential oil and many Band-Aids from daring to take a rosebud off without my protective armor.

It is pretty difficult to get fragrant roses without thorns. That is just part of the mystery of how our Lord made life. And, I believe roses will not have thorns in heaven.

MY ROSE LOVE STORY

*The heart of the rose holds
no grudges as it sweetly releases
its perfumed essence to all.*

Roses have been a special part of my life since I was a little girl living in the San Bernardino Mountains. My mom, dad, myself, and my little sister would go visit my grandparents who lived in Rancho Cucamonga, California. It was a rare treat for my sister and me to be left there with them, as my parents went off to do what parents do without little ones for a few precious hours.

I still vividly remember those visits with my grandparents. Grandpa Pettit was a real character with his big and booming voice and husky laugh. He was loved by everyone, and everywhere he went all those around heard his booming heartfelt salutations. I loved getting his big grandpa bear hugs. He had a genuine love for his family and for his roses. His large, weathered hands were gnarled by the hard work of his life, and yet he tenderly cared for his roses.

Grandpa grew those California roses to share his love for Grandma. He would pick them and bring them into their clean and simple little home. To this day, I can remember the sweet fragrance of roses when I walked into their home. I was so amazed and intrigued by the roses Grandpa grew for Grandma Pettit. I can still smell those roses in vases in the small sitting room.

What a special treat it was for grandpa to hold my hand

as he took me out to his tidy and trimmed small rose garden. As a little girl, I remember looking up at the hot summer sun, standing under those tall rose bushes, and drinking in their sweet fragrance. To this little three-year-old heart, this was a tiny piece of heavenly sunshine bringing out the magnificent heavy rose fragrance and the beautiful colors of the rose petals and shiny green leaves. This small paradise was food for my creative soul.

Yes, right there, under the sun in the rose garden, I fell in love.

It was here, at my grandparent's humble home in smoggy southern California that I fell in love with roses. Yes, right there, under the sun in the rose garden, I fell in love. I felt my grandpa's love for God, my grandma, and my family. I knew these special roses were something extraordinary. Though my grandparents were quite poor, I felt like princess in my dear grandpa's rose garden and care. I was filled with the sweetest of memories and fragrance. I determined I too would grow up and grow lots of roses to savor and also give away.

That is exactly what I did. I grew up, and in time, I had over two hundred roses bushes in my garden to love and care for. Oh! I was blessed to have so many lovely rose blossoms to give away. I even grew them commercially for a short time for local florists. That was many years ago. I now live in a banana belt in Hells Canyon with over fifty rose bushes. I get to share them with any and all who come to visit me.

THE ROMANCE OF THE ROSE

Roses are mystical.
Roses evoke emotion and passion.

ROSES ARE THE QUEEN OF HEARTS
IN LOVE, BEAUTY, AND ROMANCE

Pick a rose; yes, pick any rose that delights your soul. Now imagine holding that delicate buxom beauty in your hand. Carefully observe the graceful curves, the intriguing colors of this delicate, carefully crafted gift from the Creator's loving hands. Now drink in her glorious fragrance. Yes, that intoxicating and sweet fragrance, my friend, is an aroma like no other. The exquisite beauty and smell of the rose are small feasts capturing all the senses going deep into your soul.

Many have felt this way about the roses. Roses have been highly prized for millennia. Prose and poetry, song and dance, books and plays— all have been written about both romance and the rose. Ancient symbols of the rose have been on banners, shields, emblems, and signet rings, on into our modern-day world of logos, cosmetics, and health aids. Roses are given in commemoration, as a gift for welcoming a new birth, or celebrating a wedding. Roses are given as a special token of love or of remembrance in death. Roses are a part of our history and our lives.

Roses are God's gift to us because they are so beautiful and so versatile. They can be enjoyed for their beauty and fragrance outside in the garden and inside the home. If grown organically, they are edible. Their essence can be captured and worn as perfume or used for healing in their very breath (or essence) in essential oils.

> *There is simply the rose; it is perfect in every moment of its existence.*
>
> — RALPH WALDO EMERSON

Roses have long been the symbol of love. In Victorian times, the type or color of the rose symbolized certain meanings. For example, a single red rose meant love. A red rose bud represented pure and lovely. A single rose of any color meant simplicity. Or a white rosebud meant innocent love.

For me, any rose, any color, and any number of roses all represent love, beauty, and respect for people. If you wish to dig into the history of rose symbolism, there is a lot of information about it on the internet and in books. We will talk about this later on.

FRAGRANCE

What's in a name?
That by which we call a rose
By any other name would smell as sweet.

— WILLIAM SHAKESPEARE

The rose fragrance can be clean and light, or it may moderately fragrant, or it can go deep into my favorite, which is the heavy Old Rose perfume. It can be like strong tea with some clove. Roses can smell complex like a fine wine with fruit, blackberry, blackcurrant, or raspberry. Some roses have overtones of myrrh or musk or have undertones of lemon or citrus or have splashes of licorice.

Rose fragrance has been captured and put into perfume bottles and into beauty and health products. The memory of the fragrance of grandpa's roses in my grandma's sitting room is a part of the fabric of my soul. What is your favorite part or memory of rose fragrance?

This fragrant rose, the Sedona, is very colorful, fragrant, and rather artsy when in its bloom is full blown.

There are countless books written on the subject of the rose and everything to do with and for roses. This book is not meant to be exhaustive in any way. The beauty of the rose is too large to capture in this book.

Even though I have had Master Gardener training, I'm in no way a scientist or a certified Master Gardener. But I am a passionate lover of roses and have won top awards for my roses at the county fairs in my life. I have grown them for decades and hope to continue on growing them on into heaven for all eternity.

I wonder what it would be like to live in a world where it was always June.

— E. M. MONTGOMERY

The Lord told me to share my heart of love with you. He has given me a real and living passion for the rose. It is my humble opinion that the rose is the crowning creation of His flowers. In my life-long passion for roses, I have gathered treasures along my journey on how to treat and grow lovely roses. And now I have this privilege and opportunity to share those jewels and nuggets of understanding in how to grow beautiful, happy, and healthy roses.

A few years ago, after my husband had gone to heaven, I was in need an encouraging glimpse of heaven's hope. The Lord was so gracious and sent me a perfect prophetic word to encourage me deep down. It had to do with the things I love, along with roses of course! If this resonates with you, claim it as yours as well as the Lord speaks from His heart:

Whenever you see
A mother bird tending to her chicks,
I want you to remember that I will provide for you
In every way you need no matter what.

Though you will have challenges,
Trust that I will provide everything you need just when you need it.

Every time you see a natural rainbow,
Know that I will always honor My Word
And never leave you nor forsake you.

I count you righteous,
And therefore you are a part of the beloved.
You are protected by Me.

Every time you see a rose,
Know that I am bringing you a supernatural bouquet of flowers
To brighten your day and remind you of the intense beauty
I placed in you and in your heart.

This timely and precious word still ministers to me. Each time I see a mother bird, I am reminded of the heavenly Father's perfect provision. The Father knows I dearly love to see the colors of His promises in the sky and anywhere. So, I have beautiful prisms to catch His glorious sun rays and scatter those precious reminders all over my home to remind me that I am always protected and loved.

With the rose, I believe He saved the best for last. To this day, no matter whether I see a single rose or a bunch of roses, I am reminded that Father God handpicked those for me. I can see Him with eyes of faith, handing me His loving supernatural bouquet to bring His love and beauty into my heart and life.

Yes, you can have those supernatural love bouquets if you want as well! Just ask for the Lord to open your eyes in the natural and to open the eyes of your heart to see into the supernatural. It is a wonderful and happy place to live and be each day. Do not be afraid to ask the Lord for such good things, as He is a good and loving friend, King, and Savior.

Love sees a rose without thorns.

— GERMAN PROVERB

It is my hope and prayer that as I carefully share my life's work on the artful grace of growing and enjoying every day roses, and that you too, will grow more in love with them and their Creator. He so loves you just as you are, and He wants your life to be filled with His beauty, His endless love, and His sweet fragrance in such a colorful and unique DNA sort of way.

ROSE BUDS OF BLESSINGS

- Roses are universally considered the Queen of Flowers to express beauty, love, and passion.

- Roses embody romance with their full petals, mystical perfume, poetic shapes, and radiant colors.

- Our Creator God wants your life to be full of beauty, love, and sweet fragrance in your own colorful and unique way.

Chapter 2

SO MANY GORGEOUS ROSES & NOT ENOUGH TIME OR SPACE

How shall you paint the canvas of your garden?
What petal paints will be in your palette?
Yes! Plant a brilliant rose here with a soft pastel over there,
Splashing their glorious color on the canvas around you
Soft petals of sweetness and beauty catching the Lord's Sonlight;
With the early morning rays extracting their heavenly fragrance.
Work hand-in-hand with your Creator
For your own unique flower painting,
Outside and in your heart.

ROSES GALORE

*Paint with artistic splashes
of beauty, color, and fragrance
in the world around you.*

Did you realize that there is almost any color, size, shape, and type of rose in today's world? Most people tend to think of the typical and beautiful, but fragrance deprived, dozen red Valentine's roses. But there is so much more in this amazing world. What a blessing to live in this time of history with so many lovely roses to plant and pick.

Roses are symbolic of all that is lovely, good, and full of love and grace in this world. I encourage you to consider growing roses if you do not already. Also, think about sharing a blossom or more, if you are able, to spread that beauty and love around you.

THE MAIN TYPES OF ROSES

God loves roses — lots of roses!

Today we have over 150 species and 1000s of hybrids. Roses come in over one hundred and fifty species. On top of that, literally thousands of hybrids come in myriads of sizes, shapes, colors, stripes, blends, and fragrances. Because there simply is no single definitive way to categorize roses, most specialists divide them into three main categories: Wild Roses, Old Garden Roses, and Modern Garden Roses.

Rosehips

God is so good to put lovely edible ornaments on His favorite flowers! Rosehips are such a specialty food for birds and people and add color as winter interest too.

WHAT MAKES A WILD ROSE

Love is much like a wild rose, beautiful and calm, but willing to draw blood in its defense.

— MARK OVERBY

Have you seen a Wild Rose? If you live anywhere near the countryside where people once homesteaded, you may see these hardy roses blooming, typically in late spring and early summer. These blooming hedges are a perfect place for little birds to nest in, honeybees to pollinate around, and small animals to make their homes.

Wild Roses tend to be exceedingly thorny and generally have simple five-petal or semi-double blossoms. Each spring or early summer these amazing roses generally have one glorious show of abundant blooms. They go on to produce fruit. The fruit is called a rose hip, generally orange, red, or sometimes purple, and they are power packed with vitamin C. The wildlife will eat them during the winter. Rosehips are edible for humans as well and are great for our skin and immune system.

Different areas here in the US have different Wild Roses growing: Dog Rose, Harrison's Yellow, Praise Rose, Sweetbriar, and Wild Rose are names of just a few. There are many more varieties around, but they all seem to have some common traits: fragrance, disease resistance, and markedly prickly thorns. They grow organically with their Creator usually the One Who tends to most of them for His good pleasure, and ours as well.

OLD GARDEN ROSES

Old Garden Roses are romanticized for their fragrance and hardiness.

Old Garden Roses have been around for thousands of years. But the currently used term "Old Garden Roses" refers to all roses that were around before 1867. La France is considered our first modern day rose, and it was hybridized and introduced in that year.

There is so much more information out there on roses and their classifications. I am only giving you a brief overview. Old Garden Roses have fragrance and stamina. They are sweet and endearing but tend to bloom only once a year. They are still around and have a romantic sweetness about them.

MODERN GARDEN ROSES

Modern Garden Roses bring us color, many more repeat blooms, and the classic urn-shaped tea-sized rosebuds.

Old Garden Roses and Modern Garden Roses are subdivided further according to hybrid and lineage. With the wonderful old vintage and garden roses added to our modern-day hybridizing, we are blessed with many types, colors, and fragrances of roses to pick from for our bouquets.

There is not enough room here to discuss all the species and hybrids of roses. There are many books out there on this and good information on the internet for deeper study. I will only discuss the most common divisions that you can purchase fairly easily in nurseries today. (You will find a list of nurseries under ROSES in the *Resources* section in the back of this book.)

MODERN GARDEN *ROSES*

CLIMBING *ROSES*

ENGLISH /DAVID AUSTIN *ROSES*

FLORIBUNDA *ROSES*

GRANDIFLORA *ROSES*

GROUNDCOVER *ROSES*

HYBRID TEA *ROSES*

MINIATURE *ROSES*

I have grown roses from all groups, but I tend to love the more Modern Garden and English Roses because of their repeat blooms and lovely fragrance.

Miniatures also hold an especially sweet spot on my heart and garden because they are so cute, little, and hardy. Climbing roses are magnificent! I have grown them in years past. I would love to grow them in my current garden, but regrettably do not have the room in my small yard.

The Hybrid Tea Roses are wonderful for their wide range of colors and repeat blooming. If a person is not familiar with roses, it is a Hybrid Tea they will most likely think of when a rose is mentioned. They typically think basic red, with the classic urn-shaped high spirally center that is lovely in the vase for Valentine's Day.

Generally, everyone sticks their nose in close hoping for a whiff of the delightful aroma of that glorious and much sought-after rose fragrance; but sadly, most modern-day tea roses have a beautiful shape but little to zilch for fragrance.

Don't you agree? When you are near a rose, it's a natural thing to bend over and take a deep breath in the rose, hoping for a trace of the rose aroma? Absolutely! It comes naturally.

When the blossom has fragrance, the seeker will close their eyes and deeply inhale the perfume no matter how faint. Then they will declare with great satisfaction, "Ah, now that smells like a rose!" And usually, it will put a smile in their heart and often a grin on their face as well.

But when that sweet fragrance is absent, the disappointed admirer will pull back and declare with regret something along the lines of, "Oh, I was hoping for some scent. Well, it is a pretty rose, but a rose really should smell like a rose." Amen.

We admire our roses for their beauty and design, yes. But we *love* our roses to have fragrance as well. And for me personally, the heavier, heady scent the rose embodies the better.

*It is the belief in roses
that makes them flourish.*

— FRENCH PROVERB

I dearly love the David Austin English Roses. David Austin is a modern English Rose breeder who has been hybridizing for almost sixty years in Great Britain. He, and now his family, have blended the incredible rose fragrance of the Old Garden Roses with the repeat blooming and colors of the Modern Tea Roses. English Roses are a romantic and fragrant mix of Old Garden Roses and Modern Tea Roses. He took the fragrance from the Old Garden Roses and the colors, form, and repeat blooming from the modern roses.

God certainly put His dewy morning kisses on this lovely, delicious smelling double cupped rose, Sister Emmanuelle.

GRAFTED VS OWN-ROOT ROSES

Own-root roses can live to a ripe old age of over 100 years.

There are two basic kinds of roses to buy: grafted and own-root. The common grafted rose stocks are in most supermarkets and garden shops. You can purchase these less expensive roses as bare-root in the early spring with no dirt or potted up in gallon pots or bigger.

GRAFTED ROSES

PROS

- ✓ Most of the modern-day roses are easy to find in any local store.
- ✓ Grafted roses are less expensive. Grafted means they have been joined to a root stock, which makes them much easier and faster to propagate and therefore less expensive.
- ✓ These roses can be sold as bare roots in the early spring. Shipping is less due to the weight without the pot and soil.

CONS

- ✗ Grafted roses can have rootstock suckers and have a tendency for disease. They are weak at the graft point and susceptible to winter kill much easier.
- ✗ When a rose that is grafted above the ground is killed during a winter freeze, it is the ground stock that comes back and, sadly, their beloved rose is truly dead.
- ✗ Over the years, I have lost many grafted roses in the winters;

- but to this day, I have lost only maybe two or three own-root roses in all of the hundreds I have grown even with temperatures dipping down to -25°F.
- ✗ Grafted roses usually last to about twenty years, and then start to become sickly and quit thriving and many times even die.

OWN-ROOT ROSES

The first year they - sleep,
The second year they - creep,
The third year they - leap!

Own-root roses are only available at specialty garden shops and rose nurseries. They are more expensive as they are carefully hand-planted and are usually grown in a greenhouse for one year before being able to grow outside on their own.

WHAT ARE OWN-ROOT ROSES?

These roses are created from growing a cutting from a parent plant, usually taking a year to grow. Because they are on their own-root stock, they have more disease resistance, hardiness, and longevity.

WHY DO YOU WANT OWN-ROOT ROSES?

Own-root roses can live up to 100 years because they always grow true to their roots. Even if they have winter kill, if they are well mulched and watered, the roses will spring up new sprouts true to their heritage. Grafted roots will die at the graft, and the root stock will come up (called suckers).

OWN-ROOT ROSES COME IN POTS

This makes them smaller than a grafted rose at purchasing and planting; but they quickly grow stronger and fuller as roots grow from the same stalk, and the shoots come up from the roots.

OWN-ROOT ROSES DO NOT GROW ROOTSTOCK SUCKERS

There is a saying in the own-root world of roses:

The first year they sleep. Oh, they seem so slow.
The second year they creep. Growing, but not very quickly at all.
The third year they leap! By now they have not only caught up, but usually outgrow the grafted roses and continue growing for years to come.

OWN-ROOT ROSES ARE MORE DISEASE RESISTANT AND HARDIER

Winter kill is less likely.

IF THERE IS WINTER KILL, THEY WILL COME BACK TRUE TO VARIETY

They have their own root system, and no suckers grow from the root stock. Remember the Wild Roses? Yes, they keep growing true to their roots, even in harsh conditions.

YES, THEY ARE MORE EXPENSIVE

They are quality roses that will give you more blooms for many more years down the road. Again, own-root roses can live up to a hundred years.

PICTURE BOOKS AND CATALOGS

*The antidote for Spring or Cabin Fever:
Pour a cup of tea, then pour over rose catalogs,
dream & make plans for your garden to come*

Over the years, I cannot even begin to count the hours and weeks I have spent pouring over rose books, catalogs, and magazines trying to decide on what type of rose and what color and size of rose! Can you relate to this? For my living rose painting out in my garden, do I want a Hybrid Tea or an English Rose? Hmmm, maybe this floribunda might be perfect; but wait, this Modern Garden Rose seems so delightful.

Oh, how I love a gorgeous climbing rose, as it is spectacular to see a wall or arch of roses. I love shrub roses; but depending on variety, they can take up more room. I love miniatures for their hardiness and ease of growing in adverse conditions.
I realize I just said, "I love" many times! This flower girl is passionate about her flowers in general and roses in particular. Are you in love with the Queen of Flowers as well?

DECISIONS, DECISIONS

*A rose speaks of love silently
in a language known only to the heart.*
— AUTHOR UNKNOWN

If you are trying to figure out which rose is the perfect match for that particular spot or what rose takes your fancy for fragrance and color, I urge you to get out and go for a walk. Take a stroll through a public rose garden and see how the roses grow in their habitat and their size and what fragrance they do or don't have and the colors. Oh, wow! This color is beautiful! Go to the rose garden at different times of the season to see how the one you had your eye on holds up in the heat of summer or near the shade of a tree.

You can also ask other rose lovers what their favorites are and why. For years, I have loved "Double Delight" for its bicolor of bright cherry red on the edges and the vanilla warm white and sometimes creamy butter center, depending on the temperatures. And the fragrance is heavenly! But even though I have had many rose bushes of the much-loved rose, it is quite stingy with its blooms.

After years of devotion, my affections have turned to the perfect warm pink and porcelain white rose: "Falling in Love." The fragrance is fabulous. The tea rose form is stunning. The picturesque bush is generous with its blooms. But beware! Oh, my goodness. This rose has wicked thorns! The strong stems have an abundance of vicious, barbed thorns. But the perfect urn-shaped fragrant buds make it worth fighting those blood-thirsty thorns. These hold up so beautifully on the bush but also last extremely well in the vase.

This book is too small to begin to discuss everything on roses. A good library or even surfing the web will give you some ideas on which roses to plant and where they will grow happily.

HOW TO SELECT YOUR BEAUTY

"Susan's Stars" five-star beauty standards: fragrance, color, size, hardiness, & blooms.

There are many different ways to select a rose. I have decided to share with you my selection process. There are so many roses and not enough energy, funds, or space to have as many as you may like at times.

I honestly have every reason to believe our desires for these sweet blooms will be fulfilled in heaven. But until that glorious time, maybe these five filters will help you decide which new rose to pick for your colorful garden canvas of growing roses.

How in the world does one select a rose to plant? It may be easier to decide what traits are important to you. What seems to appeal to your soul with a rose? Is it the color, or maybe the fragrance, or even what type that makes you happy?

When I am rose shopping, I have my little shopping list filled out. Then, I start doing the research for what it is that I am looking for. For example, last fall, I knew I wanted to plant a golden yellow

English rose. There are several available on the market, and so I use this list to make the delightful selection process easier. My goal is for each rose to make all the five points.

✓ #1 FRAGRANCE

Mmm, my most favorite part of the rose is that magnificent and fabulous perfume that can greet your nose even before your eyes may see it. Yes, for me, I just must have heaven's signature scent in my roses. Why else would we be going to such lengths to grow such a flower, when we can nurture much easier growing flowers without such a fuss?

Here are some questions to consider while determining which rose is the right one to plant in your garden:

- **Does this rose you are considering have a scent?**
- **If it claims to have fragrance, what level of fragrance does it have?**

Some roses pour out light fragrance. Many roses have a moderate scent. And some have a heavy rose charm.

- **What sort of fragrance tickles your fancy?**

Some blossoms smell like berries or fruit, while others have some spice or licorice, and yet others have a resemblance to fine wine. (Isn't it just such a gift that our loving Creator gave many of His lovely roses His signature fragrance that is unique to that rose and for our enjoyment!)

✓ **#2 COLOR**

The second most important feature on my checklist is color.

- **What color do you love or what delicious blends of hues does your soul delight in?**
- **What colors are begging to be planted outside in your living canvas and soon brought inside your home to be admired or shared with others?**
- **Do you want to create a symphony of similar colors or a masterpiece with every sort of color and shade?**
- **What will look nice next to the existing plants around your baby rose?**

✓ **#3 SIZE**

- **How big is the spot where this rose will to be planted, and what are the minimum and maximum space measurements?**
- **Will it be a mini that often just needs a few inches, or a climber, pillar, fountain, or shrub rose that might grow many feet both wide and tall?**
- **Will the full-grown rose sit comfortably in her new spot or have to fight for light, air, and food among her companions?**

✓ **#4 HARDINESS**

- **How disease resistant is it?**
- **How hardy is it for your growing area?**

- **Which growing zone will allow the rose to grow most comfortably?**

Here in Washington State, I look for a rose that will grow in Zone 5. If you do not know what zone the rose grows well in, you can ask the nursery or grower you are purchasing it from. Most rose growers state the Growing Zone they will grow right in the rose description.

✓ #5 BLOOMS

- **How often will the rose bloom and how many blooms will you get?**
- **Is it one that is in continual bloom, or does it just give you a one-time spectacular display?**
- **What type of bloom am I looking for?**
- **Do you prefer a refined, picture-perfect, tight-petaled, urn-shaped hybrid tea?**
- **Or, maybe you like the romantic or English roses that are full of petals more like a peony?**
- **But then would you prefer a whole cluster of open single-petaled roses on one branch much like the Wild Roses?**

Oh, so many beautiful choices and not enough time, money, and space. But in heaven— oh, the choices that await us!

THE HUNT BEGINS

Part of the pleasure in the pursuit of the prized rose is in the hunt.

Once you have decided on which roses you are adding to your yard, you may have some challenges finding a nursery that sells that rose. I prefer own-root roses because they are so much hardier as you know by now.

The popular own-root varieties tend to sell out more quickly. If you absolutely want a certain rose cultivar, many times you may need to be on a waiting list. So, order your roses early! Many times, it is great to order in the fall for the following spring.

Own-root beauties are more expensive to buy. They are slower for the first year to bloom. But with abundant patience and love, planted in a great hole, given lots of water, showered with kind words and thoughts and prayers for God's hand of blessing over them, they are so worth the extra money, time, and work! When those roses are three years old and older, they will far outshine a grafted rose any day from that time forward.

sweetness

love and kisses

goodness

health

blessings

This is my darling grand puppy, Lily. She is my daughter's Goldendoodle, and she came to visit grandma and the posies. She just flopped down among the pansies and seemed to beg to be painted.

ROSE BUDS OF BLESSINGS

- How to decide which rose is right for you, the spot, and your garden all depends on your taste and your space.
- Order your own-root roses early, before they sell out.
- Patience is a virtue with own-root roses.
- They are slow to start but can thrive for a lifetime with proper care.

The first year they - sleep.
The second year they - creep.
The third year they - leap!

Chapter 3

COMPOSING YOUR VIBRANT ROSE CANVAS WITH COLOR & FRAGRANCE

SYMBOLIC MEANINGS OF ROSE COLORS

Red - beauty & romantic love
Yellow - friendship & cheer
White - purity & innocence
Soft Pink - sweetness & grace
Pink - elegance & happiness
Deep Pink - gratitude & thank you
Peach - sincerity & sympathy
Orange - fascination & desire
Burgundy - deep passion
Lilac - love at first sight
Purple - enchantment & mystical
Deep Purple - admiration & royalty

SEVEN YEARS OLD

Our Majestic Master Gardener designed His world with much color, design, and fragrance.

When I was seven years old, we moved from Washington State to Idaho. Even then I knew that I wanted to learn to really grow things and have a great green thumb like my mom. In my young heart, I believed she could grow anything. Now, this grownup heart still believes my dear mom can grow anything! She amazes me.

At a young age I was not good with inside plants. My family used to kid me that I could kill anything green, even an air fern. Well, it was true. As a child I just was not so good at the whole plants-need-water-to-live sort of thing. If your thumbs are not so green, believe me, there is hope! We can change.

Now I seem to be a sort of plant hospital or rescue home for sick and dying plants judging by how many plants that have been dropped off with, "I am sure if anyone can rescue this poor little plant, Susan, you are the one who can revive it." With that, these dear folks somehow seem to believe their struggling plants are in good hands and also out of their hair.

We lived in Idaho for a few years. When I was in third grade I was scared and excited to join a 4-H club in Art and Gardening projects. At this time this was all that I really wanted to commit to. Funny enough, decades later, I am still working with my art and gardening, as you hold this book in your hands and see with your eyes.

The 4-H Gardening Club was taught by a wonderful elderly lady in a tiny old home. Since I was super shy, I was relieved to realize only one other kid had signed up for gardening. That meant I got to ask lots of questions, and I always had lots of them. (So much so that my mother told me more than once she hoped that I had ten children just like me. Hmm, she must have meant it as a compliment!)

My dear 4-H leader was so patient. She kindly taught what my little seven-year-old mind could take in. It was such a thrill for me plant tomatoes and zinnias and then actually get to eat the tomatoes I had planted and pick the colorful zinnias! Oh, I still love colorful zinnias to this day.

I learned that I *could* really learn how to grow plants, and that made this young gardener incredibly happy. My patient leader planted seeds in this second grader's heart that are still alive, thriving, and bearing lots of fruit today.

Blessings to all of you out there that step up to help today's young people. You never know which ones have good soil or how much fruit they will bear in their older years. Gardening can take many years of patience and hard work to really see the results, and much more so in investing in other lives.

FOURTEEN YEARS OLD

Oh Mom, may I please, pretty please, have a rose of my very own?

When I was about fourteen years old, I had asked my dear rose-loving mother if I could please, pretty please, plant and grow a rose of my very own? My mom is exceptionally good with roses. All of my life I have seen her grow the most beautiful roses, and she continues to grow lovely roses to this day.

Mom didn't answer for the longest time. She is a careful sort of person, and she wanted me to realize what a responsibility it would be. She painstakingly told me how much work they were and that this wasn't something to take on lightly because a rose keeps on growing year after year.

Oh, how I wanted my own rose bush! I loved my Grandma and Grandpa Pettit's roses, and I was absolutely determined to not give up.

Mom and Dad were exceptionally good at teaching my sister and me good work ethics and responsibility. Dear Mom questioned if I was really ready to take on this on. Good moms are like that, and I am eternally grateful.

After planting the rose seed of a real hope, and me waiting a long time (sort of patiently), Mom finally decided YES! Was I elated!! I got to have my very own rose bush! You would have thought I had just won some great prize by my jubilant heart.

Mom went on to make it unquestionably clear that I could have my own rose *IF*:

1. I would be totally responsible to take good care my rose.
2. Continue to good care of my cat, horse, rabbits, and fishing worm business.
3. Do my share in caring for the big family garden, yard, and orchard we planted.
4. Maintain my part in helping to build our new log home.
5. Keep up my schoolwork.
6. Go on with my part-time after school janitorial job to help pay for my schooling.

Yes, of course I could and would do those all things! In my young heart, I felt a rose would be easier than my horse, pets, and my household duties. Those were easy for me by now.

Yep, I agreed. Game on, and I would get this, and it has continued to now. Ahhhh, finally getting to care my own rose! Now that sounds like heaven to me.

I was blessed with a loving and caring mom that would help me in my love of growing outside plants and roses. She taught me how to plant, care, water, weed, and tend to my plants. Mom and Dad were so gracious to give me a little bit of dirt to grow my plants to make my heart happy. Now, I get to share that love with you and whomever the Lord sends along.

MY FIRST ROSE

He who wants the rose must respect the thorn.

— PERSIAN PROVERB

As a child I was called "Suzy Sunshine." I was optimistic and loved being outside. I have always been a color lover, and sunshine yellow was my favorite color all the time I was growing up. Now my favorite color is still golden yellow but along with royal purple.

Mom generously said that I could pick out my first rose. So, with childlike exuberance, Suzy Sunshine began to pour over the rose catalogs and carefully considered each rose. Back then, the only thing I knew to pick out a rose for was its name and colors.

What rose would you pick if you only had one to select? Now that I have grown hundreds of them, it is still not easy to choose which royal rose to bring into my court of roses. As I write this, I planted ten own-root roses this spring, hoping one of these baby roses will be spectacular!

After several weeks of much debate, I finally made my first selection of the perfect rose. My child heart's desire was a multi-colored grandiflora rose called *Sundowner*. True to its name, it was full of vibrant sunset colors, with warm golds, apricots, and salmon. I was so happy to finally get a chance to develop my green thumb as I carefully tended to my newest pride and joy, my very own rose.

This brilliant sunset colored rose is Sundowner and my first rose that I owned and grew as a girl. Can you see why I fell head-over-heels in love with roses for their beauty, color, and fragrance?! Yes, I am love-struck for all eternity.

Sundowner became the first of hundreds and to this day I am an ardent lover and grower of roses. Now I have grown a pallet of glorious sunset colors in my roses and shall continue to enjoy growing roses on into eternity. On a side note, Sundowner is still available today.

START WITH A DREAM AND A VISION FOR YOUR CANVAS

These are all things to consider when you select your roses:

- **Where is your lovely plot of rose paradise to be?**
- **What environment needs does it have?**
- **What colors do you want?**
- **What sort of fragrance do you want?**
- **How much time do you have?**
- **Are they something you want to simply enjoy with minimal care, or do you want to be out primping and pruning your beauties?**

UNDERSTANDING ROSES

*Of all the flowers,
me thinks a rose is best.*

— WILLIAM SHAKESPEARE

SUNSHINE AND SHADE

Roses need many things to thrive, but sunshine is right near the top with 6–8 hours of light. For them to really thrive, they need 8–10 hours of sun. Happy roses that produce abundant, colorful, and fragrant blossoms need sunshine, rich organic soil, plenty of water, lots of food, and, surprisingly, love. Yes, I am convinced roses, and all plants for that matter, respond to our words and actions. Loving words and care engender healthier and happier plants.

Roses planted in shade tend to have weak necks that won't hold up their blooms. Also, the shade cuts down on the number of blossoms they produce. One serious issue with too much shade is that the leaves tend to be more disease prone such as powdery mildew and black spot. If you must plant them in a shady spot, the rose catalog or your local nursery will let you know which roses can be grown in lighter shade.

HEAT

Generally speaking, warmer temperatures tend to bring out more hue and vibrancy to the rose blossoms. But weather that is too hot can sun bleach and fade the colors. Again, check your local nurseries for suggestions of roses that grow well in your area.

Roses like heat but not usually direct hot sun. If you live in hot places that get high temperatures in the summer, select a rose that will hold up in the intense heat. Usually, the rose grower will note that a particular rose does well in the south or heat. Typically, roses have smaller blooms and less color in intense summer heat.

This past summer, we had a record-breaking summer for hot temperatures here in Hell's Canyon. The roses were pretty stressed most of the summer, but they seemed to bounce back going into the cooler temperatures in the fall.

HARDINESS ZONE

Growing the right rose in your zone will bring much better success. Growing the right rose for your Hardiness or Planting Zone make your job as rose gardener much easier. The Lord has been so good to have me live in a banana belt in the Lewis-Clark Valley. I live at the mouth of Hells Canyon, and it is a 7b Hardiness Zone. We have average cold temperatures of 5° F to 10°F; although, on rare occasions I have seen it down to -20°F.

But if you apply my special secrets on how to plant and grow your lovely roses, it will help keep them stay protected and safe through most winters. In all my decades of growing roses, I have rarely lost a rose to a winter kill. You can Google your growing zone or ask your favorite plant nursery. When you shop for roses, the rose specifications will usually say which zone they thrive in.

COLD WINTERS

Roses are generally quite happy in Zones 6–9. This is because the winter temperatures are not terribly cold, but if you live in Zones 3–5, you need to be much more particular about which roses you plant. You may want to consider a hardy species such as an old-fashioned, a miniature, or an heirloom rose rather than the more popular but delicate hybrid tea rose.

One of my favorite songs is not surprisingly *The Rose*. The last verse goes well with this part of caring for roses:

> When the night has been too lonely
> And the road has been too long
> And you think that love is only
> For the lucky and the strong
> Just remember in the winter
> Far beneath the bitter snows
> Lies the seed that with the sun's love
> In the spring becomes the rose.
>
> THE ROSE LYRICS
> © WARNER-TAMERLANE PUBLISHING CORP.,
> THIRD STORY MUSIC, INC.

WIND

Again, selections that are good for cold winters are also better choices for windy climates. The wind will dehydrate the rose canes and leaves. Much wind can also break or damage their canes, and then you will lose your precious blooms.

You can help protect your roses by planting them near a fence or a structure. It will help break the wind currents and give them support too. You can wrap them in burlap for winter protection as well.

All these elements need to be considered for long-term rose care. In the next chapter I share "Susan's Steps for Simply Scentsational Success with Roses."

ROSE BUDS OF BLESSINGS

- Composing your rose canvas of color, fragrance, and light creates much needed patience.

- Let your creativity flow from your heart and mind's eye and out into your yard and rose garden.

- Have fun, and know that you have a shovel and will travel to paint your rose canvas just how you want it.

This lovely red rose was trimmed with His frosty kisses in December. Normally, my roses aren't blooming this late in the year, and so it was an incredible treasure to this rose-lover's heart. A perfect heavenly Christmas present, don't you agree?

Chapter 4

SECRETS FOR GROWING STUNNING ROSES TO TURN BOTH HEADS & NOSES

*Won't you come into my garden?
I would like my roses to see you.*

— RICHARD BRINSLEY SHERIDAN

THE CROWN WEARS THORNS

"Thorns and roses grow on the same tree."
— TURKISH PROVERB

Which way do you prefer to see it? Some marvel that the exquisite rose has been created to have such vicious thorns. Others feel that God has been so good to give those thorns their beautiful roses. So, what is your perspective? I am generally optimistic because I know the Creator behind the magnificent rose, and He is the Rose. So, I see the Lord has made the rose and the curse of sin has brought on the thorns.

As I am writing now, we have just entered into the week of Passover 2020. In a few days, we will be celebrating Easter and observing our precious Lord's death and resurrection in our own homes due to a worldwide quarantine because of the coronavirus crisis. Interestingly, corona means "crown."

> *When they had twisted a crown of thorns, they put it on His head, and a reed in His right hand. And they bowed the knee before Him and mocked Him, saying, "Hail, King of the Jews!"*
>
> — MATTHEW 27:29

The Son of God, the Light of this world, wore a crown of thorns as He hung on the cross for you and me. Yes, those thorns were a corona on Jesus, the Light of the World. The crown of thorns was driven deep through His skin and into His scalp, and the life-giving red, crimson blood began to flow. He gave His blood and life in exchange for death, so that you and I have the hope of salvation from our sins. His blood also gives us the hope of eternal life as we ask Him to be our Lord and Savior.

> For God so loved the world that He gave His only begotten Son, that whoever believes in Him should not perish but have everlasting life.
>
> — JOHN 3:16

He is the Rose that was trampled for you and me. But God, in His great love and mercy, raised Jesus up out of the grave on Easter morning 2,000 years ago. The only One True and Perfect Rose was crucified, buried, and rose up from the grave giving us the free gift of eternal life if we will only, by faith, reach out and receive the gift.

In between the beginning of Passover and Easter, I had a birthday. God is so good to me, and even though I couldn't be with anyone physically this season, the Lord was so kind and loving to send me birthday gifts and cards in the mail. All these loving cards and gifts are mine because they have my name on them. I just have to receive them. They were freely given to me, and they become mine when I open them up and claim the free gift as mine.

> For by grace you have been saved through faith, and that not of yourselves; it is the gift of God.
>
> — EPHESIANS 2:8

The same is true with receiving the gift of salvation; we just have to reach out in faith and receive Jesus Christ into our heart. It was super hard and painful for Jesus, but He made it easy for us to receive the free gift into our hearts and lives. The incredible thing is this: the gift of salvation is free to us; and if we chose with our will by faith to receive that free gift, we get to live forever in heaven totally surrounded in complete love, joy, light, and peace.

Tragically, many will not receive His life gift of salvation, and because of that will be separated from the Lord Jesus forever. Please, please! Choose the free gift of salvation today! Eternity is an incredibly long time. Choose the Rose of Sharon and His gift of eternal life, love, beauty, and light. See the back of the book for a simple prayer of salvation.

The rose thorns draw blood to protect it.

*The Rose – King Jesus –
chose to wear a crown of thorns,
so His blood would protect and cleanse
us from eternal sin and death.*

NOT ALL ROSES ARE CREATED EQUAL

Now, back to growing our delightful roses here on earth; it is my hope to give you some real and practical ideas. Roses can get a bad rap as being too fussy and difficult to grow. Yes, some are pouty and fussy and prone to diseases and other issues. But many lovely roses are not difficult.

Do your research. Talk with your local nursery and check out rose reviews online and find out which roses grow well in your area. I have found that if you do your investigation and get the right rose for the right place, it will pay off when you have traffic-stopping roses!

There are so many things to know about roses. Even my own experiences of forty years of growing them cannot be put in this chapter, but I will try my best to hit the top notes and suggestions I have gathered. I will be sharing with you what I have found to work very well for me here in the Northwest.

One more reminder: I would encourage you to grow more than one rose. Roses love company, and I feel they look their best with other lovely companions. You may be wise and not go hog wild, like I did, having over two hundred in my rose garden at one time. But even three to five bushes make a wonderful group. Not all roses bloom at the same time, so with others blooming, I usually have some to pick and share or bring into my home and studio. It is a personal delight to have fresh roses all throughout my home when they are blooming. So, let's read how to get those gorgeous blooms.

This special bush, Day Breaker, sits happily near my studio windows, and is a colorful reflection of God's glory and in the early sunlight.

SUSAN'S STEPS FOR
SIMPLY *SCENT-SATIONAL* SUCCESS
WITH ROSES

Make a wish list of all the roses you want, and then go from there.

Decide which beauties you want to grow and where. I always draw my new planting map out noting the colors and expected mature height and width. I have found own-root roses take about four years to reach the maximum size with some exceptions like climbing roses and Old Garden Roses. My struggle is always how I can get as many roses as possible yet not overcrowd the blooming beauties.

ORDER YOUR ROSES

Put your rose order in early, usually in the fall, for the next spring.

Select and purchase or order your roses based on your growing conditions and what sort of rose you would like to grow and love. A word to the wise: if you have decided to get own-root roses, they are generally more available in the fall. If you have your heart set on a specific rose, I encourage you to order it in the fall and to be shipped after your frost date in the spring.

Many times, sadly, I have waited until spring to order, and the nursery was sold out. So, I either had to take my second choice or wait until the fall to try it again.

THE SECRET RECIPE

*Feed the soil
and the soil feeds the rose.*

Over the many decades of growing beautiful roses, many people have asked me, "So what is your secret recipe to grow such lush and fragrant roses?" That always brings a smile to my face, as I think back. My mind wanders back to the hours of back breaking work for the love of my roses.

As you know, any real passion has a price to pay. Also, if there is passion, there is a willingness to work hard in ways that defy human reasoning. Oh, the things we do for our love and passion.

The love of roses has caused me to dig in deep into piles of stinkin' manure or search out acres of horse pasture with a wheelbarrow and shovel for those precious horse biscuits that roses crave. In my mind's eye, I see myself like a mad woman raking up literally tons of fallen leaves to shred for mulch, and… well, you will read more about that later.

Just realize that any sweat equity put into any lovely rose gardens has come at a great cost. But the reward— that has been out of this world as well! Getting to share the roses with loved ones and strangers alike has brought me more joy than you can imagine. It is dreaming of how this baby rose or that newly transplanted rose will bloom their little hearts out for their Creator, and His beloved people that spurs me on with great hope of the future lovely bouquets to grow and share.

So, my top secret may be a surprise to you. It doesn't really have so much to do with the rose bush. It has to do with *the soil!*

#1 Top Secret

FEED THE SOIL AND THE SOIL FEEDS THE ROSE

I think I can hear some of you raise questions along the lines of, "What in the world? Ah, come on, how does feeding the soil work when you should be feeding the rose?"

After many years of practice, and planting several hundred roses, I believe this is the most important advice I can give you.

Feed the soil and that soil feeds the rose.

When I took my Master Gardener's training, I remember the instructor was adamant that you feed the soil, and the soil will feed the plant. Yes, it is absolutely true. When you have carefully fed the soil lots of good organic food, it beckons the microorganisms that are living in the soil to come alive and work with you and your bushes for years to come.

Rich organic matter also calls the night crawlers and red wiggler worms to wriggle and move through the soil. This causes the soil to open up small passageways for the air, food, and moisture to come down to the feeder roots on your roses. It makes for an especially happy micro-climate in your garden.

The secret is in the dirt:

*Put a $1 plant in a $10 hole
and you will grow a $50 plant.*

*Put a $1 plant in a $1 hole
and you might grow a $5 plant (at best) over time.*

Feed the soil and the soil will feed your rose. Our Creator made soil flourishing with life. Keeping your soil well fed with organic natural materials will keep all the living micro-organisms feeding your roses and plants for years to come.

If you just feed the rose, there is a good chance that you will greatly damage your soil. Most commercial fertilizers contain harsh chemicals that kill the tiny workers of the soil— the micro-organisms.

Roses work hard to bloom. They are voracious eaters and heavy drinkers; so to get them to really produce, feed them good organic food and give those productive beauties lots of water. They will grow beautifully and multiply and pay back in abundance.

My little sister and I raised rabbits when we were kids. We also raised and sold worms to the fishermen on the Columbia River. We grew the worms under our rabbit hutches to take care of their never-ending manure pellets. We learned first-hand at a young age that organic garden and kitchen waste would feed those red wigglers. In turn, the worms worked the rabbit pellets, garden, and kitchen waste and turned it into rich black-gold— aka compost.

Feeding the soil means feeding the garden tillers that aerate the soil. Chemical fertilizers would kill off our little gardener workers. To this day, I go as natural and organic as possible to feed the soil and my roses, and I urge you to do the same. Your roses, plants, soil, and soil workers will all thank you.

> *Do not watch the petals fall from the rose with sadness, know that, like life, things sometimes must fade, before they can bloom again.*
> — ANONYMOUS

    I wish to add a note on amending the soil with good organic materials. Amending the soil just means you are mixing nutritious materials into your dirt. This will help your plants' roots grow easier and deeper to take in the nutrients and moisture needed to thrive. It also helps your roses to grow stronger and have an easier time fighting off disease and problems.

    This last year, thankfully, I didn't have to spray my roses one time for any disease or bugs. I have faithfully fed my soil, and so my roses are full of life and joy for all to enjoy. Healthier and happier roses tend to be disease-free. And that, my friend, means you will have more time to enjoy your lovely roses instead of caring over them. The rose gardener and the roses will be happier in the long run.

#2 Top Secret
PRUNE TO KEEP YOUR ROSE CLEAN

Plain and simple, they are best kept clean for happy and healthy roses. As their petals fall, keep their feet clean to discourage bugs from taking up residence near your rose.

Some like to prune their roses in the fall. I will cut back a very long stalk that may break in the wind. We can get high winds and below zero temperatures, occasionally some winters. So, I do 99 percent of my pruning in the spring when the forsythia starts blooming. It is a perfect time to prune as we don't get a late-killing frost once the forsythia begins blooming, and it has worked very well for decades for me.

Here in Hell's Canyon, I generally prune the first couple of weeks in March. Then, with all of the crazy weather changes, I wait until I see that lovely fresh yellow bush blooming, and I know I had better get my roses pruned.

I like to keep my spring cleaning and pruning super simple:

1. Trim to shape the bush.
2. Prune out ALL diseased wood— to the ground if need be.

Spring pruning is simply cutting out all the dead, old, or weak wood. Clean off all of last year's leaves to clear out disease, and finally shape your beauty into a lovely rose bush. You and your roses will be happier all growing season.

The photo shown to the left is my spring pruning work on a Grande Dame. She is my gorgeous hot pink Hybrid Tea that has fabulous Old-World fragrance. She is vigorous, and easily grows to 6 to 7 feet tall by 6 feet wide every summer. As you see here, I prune her back to about 18 to 20 inches tall. It keeps her healthy and happy, and I love using her heavenly fragrant blossoms for the most rosy Rose Petal Jam.

3 Top Secret
LOVE YOUR ROSE

Love Jesus with all your heart and your roses will love you both back with all of their heart.

Now, this second bit of sage advice on growing fabulous roses will not make much sense at first either, but it is true, and it works. Yes, it is all about love. Love is a beautiful growing secret. Think about it; roses are all about love. They represent love in every way. They are beautiful, they smell beautiful, they are given as a symbol of love, and I believe they respond to love as well.

This world was created by love. Elohim is our Mighty Creator, and He is love! Love truly created each particle and every part of creation. All of creation was created respond to the Creator of love.

God is love.

Jesus is God the Son, and He loves you and all of His creation. When love is present, creation can't help but respond. There is ongoing scientific research on this subject. Love changes people, animals, and also plants. The Lord has written in His Word that the greatest of all is love.

> *And now abide faith, hope, love, these three; but the greatest of these is love*
>
> — 1 CORINTHIANS 13:13

So, if you carry true love in your heart, love on Abba Father God. Love on Jesus, your Savior, and the Lover of your soul. Love on your roses. Guess what? Your roses will love you back. Indeed! I know this to be true as I have seen it in my own rose garden for many, many years.

There are times when I go out to love on my plants. I literally feel like a conductor of a fine orchestra. I tell my dear roses to sing and dance for Jesus. I encourage them to lift up their branch arms, and smile at their Creator as they smile with their lovely rosy faces and sing His love song back to Him.

I tell their roots to sing and dance as well. It creates waves of delight, joy, and love in my heart whenever I do this, and it can be literally sensed in the garden. Many visitors have commented on the peace and fragrance of this place just stepping out of their car on the street.

Believe it or not, there have been visitors that have come to visit my roses, and they have exclaimed how the roses are singing with the little flower angels, the birds, and the bees buzzing. All of creation wants to join in the chorus of love and adoration to the King.

For you shall go out with joy, And be led out with peace; The mountains and the hills Shall break forth into singing before you, And all the trees of the field shall clap their hands.

— ISAIAH 55:12

On a side note: I don't usually say this so the whole neighborhood will hear me; and yes, my neighbors do wonder about me at times, I am sure. But it is all good, and it's a happy and peaceful place. So, I sing or speak softly to the roses and plants, and I am convinced the roses listen with their hearts.

My conclusion is this: as you send out your love for the Lord God, and for your roses; they will worship their Creator with beautiful love. Their lovely affection is shown is charming blossoms, stunning beauty, striking color, and heavenly fragrance.

Roses are all about the love.

I believe the rose is the Lord's favorite flower for so many reasons, and I certainly wouldn't disagree, would you?

ROSE BUDS OF BLESSINGS

- Do your research.

- Talk with your local nursery and check out rose reviews online to find out which roses grow well in your area.

- Remember this #1 top secret: feed the soil, and you feed the rose, and all will grow much better.

- The # 2 top secret is that roses represent love and they respond to love.

Amazing Grace, how sweet the smell that drew my heart closer to my Creator God! This robust globular rose, full of fragrant petals, and delicious color, will turn any mouth into a smile with delight at the full fragrance and velvety petals.

Chapter 5

ENERGETIC ROSES LOVE ORGANIC MEALS & COMFY BLANKETS

A little fragrance always clings to the hand that gives the roses.

— A CHINESE PROVERB

FROM THE GROUND UP

> *But he who received seed on the good ground is he who hears the word and understands it, who indeed bears fruit and produces: some a hundredfold, some sixty, some thirty.*
>
> — MATTHEW 13:23

You want good soil and beautiful roses. It all starts in the ground with the dirt. Just like God took some clay from the Garden to form Adam. He knew it was in the dirt. There is microscopic life in the ground under your feet. If you treat it well, it will help you get the great return on your investment of labor, money, and time in the plants you grow.

Now, we are going to get into the nitty gritty dirt about planting those traffic stopping roses. It literally begins with digging a good hole and feeding that hole lots of great organic food for a healthy rose. Let's dig in!

TOOLS FOR THE TRADE

To plant your lovely newest baby rose, you will need some tools to help:

- Good, sharpened shovel to dig with: which makes digging the large hole so much easier
- Good pair of leather gloves: I prefer goat skin as it is incredibly soft and offers good protection
- Wheelbarrow: to mix your soil amendments, haul off extra soil
- Long sleeved shirt: to protect your arms from thorns and the sun

- Small hand trowel or claw: to mix in the soil amendments
- Knee pad: to save your weary knees
- Water hose: to water in your rose
- Hose-end nozzle sprayer
- Large watering can
- A good quality pair of sharp hand pruners

WARNING

Do not be deceived, God is not mocked; for whatever a man sows, that he will also reap.

— GALATIANS 6:7

Yes, you can go out and purchase an inexpensive rose bush, dig a hole, plant it, and water it. And yes, it will grow. And I am guessing many roses are planted this way each year. And to be perfectly honest, some will grow and do well for a while, while others will quickly shrivel and die.

But most roses won't thrive with just sticking them in the ground and watering. Simply put, you reap what you sow, and you will get more of whatever you put into the process.

In order to get big, colorful beauties that will flourish and amaze, you have to make an investment of your time, energy, resources, and muscle into them. With roses, and a lot of other things, you will reap more than what you invest.

It is a universal truth because God is a Creator and a Gardener. You reap what you sow. A real harvest is a lot more that what you had planted, whether good or bad. For example, if you plant one sunflower seed, water it well, and care for it; you will get lots of sunflower blossoms and countless seeds at harvest.

Rose gardening is along the same principle. If you have chosen to plant a good bush and put in the effort and expense to plant it well, you will reap countless flowers for many years to come.

Growing lovely roses is not for wimps. It takes brawn to get those beauties to produce. But two to three years later, your hard work in giving them a good hole to grow in will pay off. Giving those babies lots of good water and care, you will be amazed at how much they will produce. They will reward you for years after your sore and tired muscles have healed.

When you plant any rose in a big hole with lots of great food, and then also pray for God's favor and grace over it, you can enjoy that rose for many years. If it is an own-root rose, you can pass that heritage down to your grandchildren!

NATURAL INGREDIENTS

Just like us, your roses are what they eat.

Feed them natural food, and they will naturally grow and flourish for you.

Please **DO NOT** use chemical or synthetic fertilizers on your new roses, or any roses for that matter. Chemicals will burn those tender rose roots and kill the micro-organisms in the soil. If you put organic supplies in your rose hole, it will give both the soil and your rose healthy food for a long-living, productive, and happy rose.

I would encourage you to never, if it at all possible, feed your roses chemicals. They are vivacious eaters, and when fed a proper natural and healthy diet, you will be blown away at how well they will shine for you!

FISH STORY

Quick story: anyone in my family knows I love the outdoors and I like to see fish, but I *love* to give any fish parts leftover from fishing trips to my roses. My long-time next-door neighbor, along with a dear ninety-six-year-old friend and cowboy, are both avid fishermen. They have both been known to bless me and my roses with extra fish and the fish innards that they cleaned out after fishing in the Snake River and surrounding lakes. These men have made me, and my blooming roses, and many happy rose recipients delighted with their thoughtful and generous fish gifts from their fishing trips.

Roses love, love, love fish in their big hole at planting. And they also appreciate a snack of fish emulsion (aka Alaska liquid fish fertilizer) on their leaves and roots during their growing season. Fish give them such healthy and happy roots, leaves, and stalks with vibrant color and more fragrance. Good stuff. If you are not blessed to live near a fishing place like I do here on the Snake River, you can buy fish fertilizer. The stinkin' stuff makes bloomin' roses flourish beautifully.

THE BIG FIVE

We will water the thorn for the sake of the rose.

— KANEM PROVERB

Along with the three top secrets, #1 feed the soil, #2 prune them clean, and #3 love your roses, I am sharing the following lists and how-tos. This is what people want to know when they ask how I am blessed to grow such full and vibrant roses. Now you will be able to grow real beauties as well. If you already grow beautiful roses, maybe there will be some new tips for you also.

When you plant a new rose, these five natural ingredients will be extremely helpful in giving you years of traffic-stopping roses on each bush:

ALFALFA PELLETS

1 pound (like sheep or rabbit food) is for trace minerals to give their deeper colors and more shoots coming up. You can get it in the farm animal section, or at a feed store.

EPSOM SALTS (MAGNESIUM SULFATE)

1/2 cup of encourages new growth and vibrant coloring. This is the same stuff that would be in the health section at your local supermarket that you soak your feet or sprained ankles in. I usually get it in 5 to 8-pound bags at Walmart.

FISH MEAL

1 pound of or 1 cup of liquid fish fertilizer, such as Alaska Liquid Fish Fertilizer. Fresh fish work too if you are able to get some. The fish meal will go at the bottom of your hole, so the neighborhood dogs and raccoons don't dig it up.

MANURE

10 to 15 pounds of 6-month aged or older. I like to feed them *aged* horse manure the best, but *6-month aged* cow or chicken will work too. Manure in pies or biscuits, like horse and cow, needs to be aged so it doesn't burn the tender roots. Droppings or pellet manures (such as rabbit, sheep, and goat) do not need to be aged.

COMPOST

Again, aged is best. It acts like a blanket while feeding the soil too. It also helps to protect your roses from drought, wind, and freezing. It acts as a weed blanket barrier as well.

EXTRA INGREDIENTS FOR THE BEAUTY AND STRENGTH OF YOUR ROSES

A thorn defends the rose, harming only those who would steal the blossom.

— CHINESE PROVERB

If you want bigger, hardier, and longer lasting rose bushes, these extras make a difference. I have found that adding these at planting gives the rose a real boost. Add the following extra favorites in addition to the "Big Five" ingredients listed above:

AZOMITE

1/2 to 1 pound to re-mineralize the soil and promote growth

COMPOST

1/3 to 1/2 of the hole filled with composted leaves and organic material to feed the soil

BANANAS

Yes, you read that right. Cut up 3 to 5 of them with the peelings on for potassium for their roots to take in

DRIED BLOOD MEAL

2 Tablespoons for greener leaves

DRIED KELP

2 Tablespoons as a good soil conditioner and for trace minerals

MYCORRHIZAE

1 ounce mixed in at the hole around the roots. Save it for the end of the planting, to go next to the new growing roots

SUPERTHRIVE

Transplanting help

DIG DEEP AND WIDE

God's Gardening Truth:
You reap what you sow.

Real gardening is hard work, as you fully realize. Even Adam and Eve, the first gardeners on earth, had to work hard at it like you and me.

If you have chosen the hard work at the beginning of your rose gardening in digging the big hole, it pays off. It is pretty sweet to reap the rewards for years to come with your beautiful roses. The Lord will be true to His Word and His principles: you will reap what you sow. It is true in the rose gardening world as well.

THE PLANTING

Planting the rose properly is both the hardest physical part of this process, and also the most important part in giving your rose a happy home to thrive. Here are the steps:

THE DIG

Digging the big hole is the deep secret to having those head-turning beauties bursting out in abundance of blooms. It takes a lot of sweat and toil at the planting stage.

Roll up your sleeves and dive in for your workout in digging an 18" x 18" hole for most roses and a 24" x 24" deep and wide hole for large shrubs and ramblers.

Digging such a large hole will ensure good drainage and allow room for adequate nutrition. Roses need good drainage so those tender roots will not suffocate and eventually die in stagnate water. A well-dug hole gives your roses lots of room so the delicate feeder roots can easily grow with the loosened soil and amendments.

THE DIRT

As you dig, set approximately 1/2 of the dirt aside to be mixed with the amendments. The other 1/2 of the dug out dirt will need to be saved separately, since part of it will be need used as "just dirt."

Mix any or all the above organic additives together with about 1/2 of the soil you dug out. I like to use the wheelbarrow for this; it makes it easier to thoroughly mix the dirt and additives together. Use your shovel to mix it well.

Adding the life-giving organic materials make a big difference. All the natural ingredients feed the soil as well as encouraging more soil activity. It also gives the soil slightly acidic conditions, which make for happy roses. The soil amendments can help clay soil loosen up and drain well and can also bring some water-retaining help to sandy soil.

THE HOLE

Dump several shovels of the un-amended soil back into the bottom of the freshly dug hole. This will loosen up the packed soil.

Next add in about 1/4 of the organically amended soil from your wheelbarrow. Mix the dirts together well. The hole should be back filled to about 1/2 the depth now.

FIRST WATER

Using your garden hose, fully water the 1/2 filled in hole all the way to the top of the hole.

Let the water drain. It will take a little time for this to happen. Go get a glass of water and take a break for a few minutes. You want the soil and amendments to get soaked and settled.

POT HOLE

Once the water is drained from the hole, set the rose in its pot in the half-full hole. Yes, you read that right. Put the potted plant in the hole.

Set the pot so the rim is 2 to 3 inches below the soil level. This is a major protection for your rose against winter kill!

You may need to add more plain soil to raise it up or dig down to set the rose in right. You may need to make some adjustments at this point to get the correct depth.

Setting the rose — still in its pot— down into the dug hole, will enable you to give you your newly planted rose protection. It will also create room for a water reservoir around your bush during the first growing year.

If you are planting own-root roses, roots will begin to grow out of the main stems as well, and they will be true to the parent stock.

THE FILL

Now, fill in just *plain dirt* (*NOT the amended soil from the wheelbarrow*) around the sides of the pot.

You do not want any fertilizer to possibly burn those roots, so the plain soil is like an insulted layer between the exposed rose roots the remaining soil with the added amendments.

SECOND WATER

Once the hole is completely filled in around the pot with plain soil, water the rose hole again and let it drain. At this point it will look like you have the rose planted; except the pot is still in the dirt.

Watering the soil again now will make sure the amendments are well moistened, and it will help remove air pockets in the soil. Once the water has soaked in, you are ready to remove the potted rose.

REMOVE THE POT

Carefully lift up the potted rose. As you remove the pot from the ground, you will be leaving a perfect hole that is the same shape as the potted plant.

SUPPORT THE ROOTS

Carefully sprinkle the powered *1 ounce of mycorrhizae* all around the bottom and the sides of the hole. This will stimulate the tender feeder roots to grow strong to help take in the nutrients needed to grow your healthy rose. It won't burn or harm the delicate feeder roots at all. I have found this one secret makes a huge difference in getting the plant to start growing quickly with little or no transplant shock.

PLANTING THE ROSE

Now remove the rose gently from the pot. This takes some patience and tender care. Gently remove the plant from the pot by turning the pot upside down and pushing on the bottom soil.

DO NOT PULL THE PLANT OUT OF THE POT. It is especially tender, and you do not want to damage the stems or roots. Gingerly slide the removed rose dirt ball.

Plant the rose bush and root ball back into the perfect-sized depression that you made in the soil. The roots should fit exactly.

TOP IT OFF

DO NOT start pushing the soil down by hand! Gently add the rest of the amended soil around the top of the plant.

THIRD WATER

Then simply water your new rose plant thoroughly with your hose-end nozzle. Let the water wash the soil into the crevices.

VOLCANO SHAPE

Build up quite a bit of unamended dirt into a raised ring around the now planted rose, so that it looks almost like a mini volcano. This creates a water reservoir for your water to go into. It will allow you to fill it up with water, and it will allow the water to slowly soak down to the roots.

I put a rather large wall of dirt and compost around all of my first-year roses. It makes it so much easier for them to drink in all the water they so desperately need as they are particularly tender and delicate for their first year.

This will help provide summer moisture for the roots. It will also give you a well to fill up with winter mulch in the fall for winter protection from winter kills in that first sensitive year. I have rarely lost roses to winterkill when I set them down just 2" to 3" below the soil level.

FOURTH WATER

Fill your watering can with water and apply the Superthrive according to directions. Water your rose bush and fill your water reservoir with the water and Superthrive mixture. This will really help minimize the risk of transplanting shock. You may need to do this a couple of times until you are satisfied the rose is watered in.

MULCHING

Put one to two inches of compost around the rose in the water ring. Use compost, dried leaves, or straw as your mulch.

Do not put it any thicker than 2 inches. The roots need protection, but it will also need the heat to grow. A thin layer will help conserve water and not allow them to dry out so quickly. The compost will give them a blanket of protection from temperature variations.

All new babies need blankets to comfort them, and baby roses are no different.

WATERING SCHEDULE

Continue to water every day for the next few weeks until you feel they are growing well.

Please be careful to only water the soil and not the leaves. **Roses don't like their leaves getting wet** as it encourages diseases.

CODDLE THEM

Continue to baby your new roses the first year with plenty of water. Next year you can treat them like the rest of your roses, but this first year is so critical, especially for own-root roses.

You may want to even put a wire cage around your rose for support and protection from children and pets as well. Wire tomato cages work well and are easy to get at any garden or hardware center.

PRAYER

Seriously, take a few moments to ask the Lord to bless your newly planted roses. Praise God for His ever-faithful love and light and ask Him to bless the little rose. Speak to the rose to lift up its branches and rosy faces to His Son to bring Him glory and praise!

    And there you have it! You now have my deep secrets of how to get beautiful blooming roses tucked into your healthy soil for a happy rose bush for all to enjoy for many to enjoy years from now.

PLAIN AND SIMPLE EVERYDAY PLANTING

Alright! So, after reading that long and exhausting list, you are thinking, "Sure thing, Miss Rose Lady; that's not going to happen here!" Well, I can certainly understand your exasperation! And so, for those of you who are limited on your time, funds, energy, and patience, I am offering you the following ultra-condensed version of planting your fantastic new rose bush:

SIMPLE PLANTING PLAN

- Dig a hole a big as you are able with your time and energy. It should be at least 4" larger than your rose pot
- Add anything from the list you want, but especially alfalfa pellets, compost, fish, or leaves
- Mix the dirt and amendments into the hole with your shovel
- Set the potted rose in the hole with the rim of the pot an inch below the soil level
- Back fill the hole in with dirt and compost
- Water the dirt around the rose in the pot and let it drain out
- Remove the potted rose and gently slide the removed rose dirt ball back into the pot-sized hole
- Gently add a shovel full of dirt around the top of the plant
- Water your new rose plant thoroughly with your hose-end nozzle washing the soil into the crevices
- Build up a raised ring of soil around the rose, so that it creates a watering ring
- Continue to water your newest rose arrival the first year with plenty of water

Praise God for His great love and light. Ask Him to bless your little rose. Proclaim over your rose that it is to lift up its branches and rosy faces to the Son so it can bring Him glory and praise!

Patience brings roses.

— HUNGARIAN PROVERB

The first year, it is super critical that you water the rose well. Do not overwater and create waterlogging but keep the soil well-watered. It has exceptionally delicate roots growing; and keeping the soil well-watered is a great way to help ensure a long and happy life.

Own-root roses take a couple of years to grow well; but by the third year, they surpass their grafted-root cousins by leaps and bounds. Then they just keep on growing well and blooming their little hearts out!

Don't forget that saying about own-root roses:

The first year they - sleep;
the second year they - creep;
the third year they - leap!

Over the years, with tremendous care with the planting, I have lost few roses. Sometimes it just happens for various reasons, but generally not so much with good planting, ample water, a fall top dressing with compost, aged manure, and one-pound of alfalfa pellets— plus my secret ingredient which I will share at the end of the chapter.

There is something quite captivating in observing how buds grow into such lovely blossoms. This is Sister Emmanuelle after a quick summer shower. She and our Creator seem to beckon us to stop and smell the roses.

MULCHING IS THE MAGIC CARPET

Today, stop, look, and drink in the beauty of summer roses; winter will be here before you know it.

Personally, weeding is not one of my favorite things to do. Now I don't mind the time and effort to deadhead, but pulling weeds, not so much. Mulch to the rescue! It is a time, money, and stress saver.

You'll soon see the benefits of mulching your rose beds as it:

- Is inexpensive
- Is attractive
- Saves water by putting a blanket over the roots to keep the water from evaporating away
- Keeps moisture in so you have to use less water
- Stays in place well around the rose base
- Acts as a sun shield, as it helps to keep your plants from getting too hot during the hot summer
- Also acts like a winter blanket to insulate the roots from winter-killing due to the freezing and thawing temperatures
- Feeds the soil as it protects the growing roots
- Easily worked into the soil
- Helps eliminate weeds as it helps to keep the weeds from sprouting, and that means less weeds going to seed
- Does not need to be removed once applied
- Easy to work other organic soil amendments in the spring, such as alfalfa pellets

- Keeps the roses clean so water will not splatter dirt up on the highly prized blossoms
- Continues to feed the soil and all of its micro bioactivity

MULCH

Mulch is both a blanket of protection and a way to have a constant source of moisture and food available. It is a great key to healthy, happy plants, and that makes you a less stressed gardener. Sounds like stuff your lovely roses may need!

The mulch and compost very much keep them blooming longer. And protect them from the heat and cold.

But what is mulch? Good question.

Mulch is like an amazing magic carpet that protects your plants year-round. It is generally, but not exclusively, comprised of organic materials that you lay it over your roses' feet. Again, going green with organic healthy foods, you can lay down the mulch of things such as:

- Aged manure (six months old or older) such as horse biscuits or rabbit pellets
- Decaying leaves: roses love both oak and maple leaves, but not walnut or pine needles due to the high acid content
- Compost material
- Landscaping bark
- Compost

Starved roses tend to be sickly and will be more stingy with their blooms. The best bloomers are well fed, well-tended, and well-watered.

What is compost? Compost is organic material that you allow to decay and become fertile "black gold" soil. I call it black gold because it is so dark in color and rich in nutrients. It feeds the soil that feeds your lovely roses. This is part of the secret in the dirt.

Compost will literally call in the hard-working worms to labor in your pile to eat and recycle the waste in your mound into glorious dirt. The red wiggler worms have voracious appetites. They will assist in speeding up the whole composting process and make it much healthier with their worm castings (worm waste.) Compost can be purchased if you don't have the time or space to create your own compost pile, BUT I personally believe roses really love home-cooked compost. It is good to always have a compost pile on your property if space can allow for it.

All year long you can add to the green machine compost pile:

- Bananas
- Citrus rinds
- Coffee grounds
- Eggshells
- Garden waste
  (not weed seeds, for obvious reasons)
- Garlics
- Grass clippings
  (not sprayed or fertilized with weed killers)
- Manure: horse or rabbit is best for roses
- Non-dairy kitchen waste
- Onions
- Tea bags

- Anything organic that will break down into dirt over time
- Even sod makes a good compost in time

Please note: DO NOT add dairy, fat, or meat into your compost. If you do, it will call in the wild things from your neighborhood that will dig through and make a mess. Those things also don't break down well for your rose compost.

A compost pile will get hot. This is part of the mysterious process that breaks down the garbage and turns it into rich soil. God is so good to give us compost for our debris. Just keep the pile watered and turned every so often with a shovel or pitchfork throughout the growing season. The water and turning will speed the composting process, keep the smell down, and mix the nutrients being processed. When the compost cools down, the waste will now become a worm-filled rich soil amendment to place in your dug holes and around your planted roses bushes and other plants as a mulch.

MULCHING TRICK

Compost simply becomes mulch when it is placed around your roses like a blanket.

My personal favorite mulching trick is best executed in the fall. This little secret helps to speed the composting time to make mulch right in your rose bed. This is not an exact science, so experiment with your rose beds to figure out what they need and works for your area. Just add a small bucket of six-month-old, or older, horse or rabbit manure around both the base and dripline of the unpruned rose bush. On top of the manure layer, add 2–3 inches of chopped fallen tree leaves. Water it in; and a year from now, it will look just like black rich soil.

Finished compost works well to mulch your roses for the winter or again in the spring, and or at planting to keep weeds down, moisture in, and the rose leaves and blossoms clean.

SPRING AND FALL FEEDING

You want well-rounded, abundant, and beautiful roses? You must feed them!

Roses are big producers. It takes a lot of sheer muscle and hard work for your lovelies to produce a vibrant and stunning display of buds and blossoms each year. They are a lot like our children, in order for them to grow well they must be well fed and watered. Just like we learned we need to feed the soil to get great results; know you must feed your rose a full meal-deal to get long-lasting and prized blooms. It takes a lot of energy to produce blossoms, and that translates to they eat a lot.

To get a stunning show time bunch of roses, feed those beauties! Feed them good amounts of a variety of beneficial foods all through their growing season. These demanding producers feed heavily on the useful food you put in their holes at planting. I realize I am repeating myself, but repetition aids in learning. Roses eat and drink— *a lot*.

Also, continue the effective care each spring and fall as you work 1 pound of alfalfa pellets into the soil around each bush, along with one ounce of Epsom salts. Working that into the soil and watering it in well is multi-tasking by feeding those hard-working earthworms, the soil, and most of all your beloved roses.

If you find that your rose leaves are light green, add iron into the soil at the recommended amount on the label. Yellow and light-colored roses seem to need iron most often each spring and many times again in the fall.

HOPE

My motto: have shovel, will travel.

Take heart, dear rose grower, if that rose you planted here would do so well in its perfect spot, and it's not thriving; know that it's certainly okay to move it. Sometimes, unexpected, good and bad things happen in the garden world. There are times we just don't understand why a plant isn't thriving as we had hoped.

So, go on and get out your shovel. Transplant the rose to a new spot.

Or, on some occasions, the absolute worst thing happens. Your lovely rose passes onto heaven's rose gardens. Groan! Dig it up, put all new soil and amendments into the hole, and plant a new one in its place.

SUPERNATURAL HOPE

*Now may the God of hope fill you
with all joy and peace in believing,
that you may abound in hope
by the power of the Holy Spirit.*

— ROMANS 15:13

True story, a few years back, I had this happen to me:

My wonderful little white rose, called Earth Angel, died! Oh, my goodness! I couldn't believe that she really died. (You will get to see her in Rose Trilogy Volume 3 with the literal angel feather on her leaves.) What in the world? I was shocked! How could this healthy and happy rose die on me? I had followed my rose instructions, you read earlier in this book.

That fall, I ordered another own-root Earth Angel. I wanted to be sure it was reserved and secure for spring delivery. As hoped, it arrived the following May. I replanted the baby rose with lots of love and prayers. I planted it with all new soil and amendments and believed for magnificent blossoms.

Well, guess what? Nooo! Not happening!

You have got to be kidding me. There is just no way I am going to accept the fact that this second bush died too! Oh boy. I was ticked off. This time, I was angry at the darkness, I was fuming at the enemy, and that evil old serpent from the Garden of Eden.

No on my watch. The Irish in me had gotten the best of me, and I was absolutely **not** going to happen let this baby rose die. No, satan, you are NOT going to win this round. I was sticking to the promise of God here:

> *The thief does not come except to steal, and to kill, and to destroy. I have come that they may have life, and that they may have it more abundantly.*
>
> — JOHN 10:10

I prayerfully went into battle mode. Got some anointing oil and put it on its frail brown and shriveled branches. Next, I literally began crying out loud to Abba Father. (Yes, sometimes my neighbors do wonder about me.) By God's grace, I was not going to give up on this little rose. The enemy of our souls would not win this battle. I believed Jesus was already the winner, and I firmly believed for a miracle from Abba Father. Speaking out loud, in the Name and blood of my All-Powerful Jesus, I commanded baby Earth Angel's precious life to return to the bush, to literally grow, and thrive with life and abundance.

Miraculously, Earth Angel did come to life, just like that. God was gracious to both of us. Holy Spirit came and breathed life into the precious tiny and very dead Earth Angel rose bush. Elohim, our Mighty Creator, brought resurrection life back into my little white Earth Angel rose through. Thank you, Jesus! I shouted and cried in sheer gratitude and joy.

> *But thanks be to God, who gives us the victory through our Lord Jesus Christ.*
>
> — JOHN 10:10

As a special token of love, Abba sent me and Earth Angel His kisses. The following year, the one-year-old bush grew another baby Earth Angel, right next to it, on the east side. That rarely happens, especially for a first year rose bush. I believe it was as if the Lord gave me back what the enemy had stolen from me. I love how our Lord God looks after us in every area of our lives.

I do have witnesses that saw this whole process, and we are still amazed and delighted to this day. These dear ones still come to check on her growth each year. As you are well aware, nothing is impossible with our God. But God, in His great love for you, me, and all His creation, delights to bring abundance in life, miracles, and wonders in our everyday lives.

Realize new plans, moving plants, and changing things out can happen to the best of gardeners, and that is okay. God promises to make all things work together for good to those who love God, to those who are the called according to His purpose. What a beautiful and life-giving promise that is.

TAKING CARE OF THE BAD GUYS

Roses fall, but the thorns remain.

— DUTCH PROVERB

So even with all the love, blessings, good wishes, hard work, and care that you pour out on your lovely roses, sometimes the bad guys come in to kill, steal, and destroy your prized rose garden. The thieves come disguised as pests and diseases like aphids, thrips, spider mites, cane borers, Japanese beetles, rust, mildew, viruses, and a host of others. Again, I try my absolute best to go organic whenever possible.

When you must spray the bad bugs, a good rule of thumb is to spray really early in the morning or late in the evening so as not to hurt the good guys, such as the beneficial hard-working insects, lady bugs, honeybees, and lacewings.

APHID AND BAD BUG SPRAY

- 1 tablespoon baking soda
- 2½ tablespoons light cooking oil, such as sunflower or canola
- 2 tablespoons mild household dish soap

1. Mix with 1 gallon of water into a gallon sprayer.
2. Apply when symptoms of disease appear.
3. Spray in early morning or late evening.

4. Be sure to spray under the leaves where many insects hide.
5. Spray every 3 days until the bugs disappear.

You can also use Safer Insect Killing Soap or Neem Oil according to the manufacturers' recommendations if you want a safe commercial spray for problem insects on your roses.

ONE MORE SECRET

Keep their feet clean, and you will have less fussing with bad bugs and disease.

Rose do best when they are kept clean. Their leaves like to be shiny clean; and spraying them every 4–6 weeks with fish emulsion gives them a good washing and a powerful energy drink in through their leaves and roots.

Make it a regular practice to go through your rose bushes and deadhead the spent blossoms. It will encourage new growth, but it will also discourage disease and bugs from deciding to take up housekeeping in your beautiful roses. Keeping your clippers clean also keeps diseases from spreading from bush to bush.

Also, when you are done deadheading, rake up or scoop up the fallen leaves and petals. Again, bad bugs love roses, and they think that the petals and leaves make a great breeding ground for more infestations. So, disease and pest-free rose bushes, by cleaning up rose beds, make happier roses that bloom with greater enthusiasm.

ENERGY DRINK

Just remember, during the winter,
far beneath the bitter snow,
that there's a seed that with the sun's love
in the spring becomes a rose.

— BETTE MIDLER

Roses love a fish flavored energy drink every 3 to 4 weeks throughout their growing season. Fish emulsion or Alaska Fish Fertilizer is a wonderful boost to get those girls bloomin' their best. Fish fertilizer won't burn the leaves or roots and gently absorbs through their leaves and roots. Yes, it is stinky for a little while, but the end results are worth making a little stink.

This is my modified recipe that I have used for years. This mixture will treat approximately 20 roses. And yes, roses love to sip on black tea as well for the tannins, as it is slightly acidic. (Hint: the roses and earthworms will love the spent tea bags at their feet when finished making the energy drink.)

ROSE ENERGY DRINK

1 garden hose sprayer

1 cup of hot water with 2 bags of black tea to make a strong tea; then remove the tea bags and cool. (Hint: sometimes I make it the night before to let it steep and cool.)

2 tablespoons mild dish soap or baby shampoo. (This will help the drink to stick to the leaves and break through the leaf tension so the rose leaves will absorb the energy drink.)

2 cups fish emulsion or Alaska Fish Fertilizer

1 tablespoon iron

1 tablespoon Epsom salts

An early morning application is best. If applied during the middle of the day, it hurts the good bugs. If applied in the evening, the moisture encourages mold and mildew.

1. Pour the cooled strong tea into the Garden Hose Sprayer.
2. Add the other ingredients.
3. Fill to the top with water.
4. Apply the sprayer to your hose end and spray your roses from top to bottom, on top of the leaves, and under the leaves.
5. Spray their roots and under their drip line as well.
6. Reapply every 3 to 4 weeks.

A SURPRISING TOP SECRET — HEAVENLY HELP

*For you shall go out with joy,
and be led out with peace;
the mountains and the hills
shall break forth into singing
before you, and all the trees of
the field shall clap their hands.*

— ISAIAH 55:12

So, I am going to share with you one of my top secrets in how to grow such healthy, happy, and flourishing roses. I think it may surprise you.

I literally pray almost daily that our Heavenly Father will bless the flowers to make people smile and stop and smell the roses. I pray that He will flourish this place for His glory and good pleasure. Seeing a whole symphony of flowers thriving together makes me so happy. I was tickled to see a few people stop by this week as I write and take pictures of my roses. Passing by they would stop on their walk and just rest, or soak in the colors and fragrance into their souls.

Several years ago, I felt that the Lord wanted me to pray that I would send His flower and waterway angels to my little cottage and garden to help tend to the flowers. I even put several dozen solar lights among the roses, as I sensed the angels would like to see the flowers better as they carefully took care of them while I slept. It was all simply done and in faith, believing somehow that the Lord had heard and answered my prayers.

> *Are they not all ministering spirits sent forth to minister for those who will inherit salvation?*
>
> — HEBREWS 1:14

One day, a couple of years ago, the roses were doing well. I also had several lilies and other flowers blooming among my roses. For whatever reason, on that delightful, late summer day, I sensed the flowers' great happiness and joy as their color and fragrance filled the air with music. It literally seemed as if all of the flowers had joined in some happy heavenly choir, with exuberance of song and dance. They seemed to be singing with sheer adoration and joy to their Lord and Creator.

As I sensed the floral celebration continuing, my dear friend stopped by my home studio, to pick up some finished commissioned artwork. I helped her carry the art out. She got into her SUV and started it. She sat there rather reflective for a moment. I was a little surprised but waited patiently for her next movement.

Then it bubbled out as she couldn't contain the joy any longer. She rolled down her car window as a brilliant smile lit up her face. With dancing eyes, she deliberately turned to me, and spoke with sparkles in her eyes, "Susan, I just have to tell you this!"

My spirit was beginning to feel an expectant heavenly rush. I excitedly clasped my hands together as I responded, "Oh, yes, please do tell!"

"I wasn't going to tell you, but it's just too funny and I must share!" as her shoulders shook jovially.

Now my curiosity was aroused, "Go on! Do tell!"

She went on to explain the joy bubbles that seemed to be floating festively all around us. "When I drove up into your driveway to pick up my finished art pieces, I got out of the car, and there seemed to be a whole lot of activity all around your home and flowers! You see, there were little streaks color zipping all over, and lots of excited whispering and a few little arguments going on out here."

"What in the world?" I asked in amazement, and not understanding what she meant.

> Let the rivers clap their hands;
> Let the hills be joyful together before the Lord
>
> — PSALMS 98:8–9A

She continued, with great delight. "Oh, yes! The frenzied activity is an entire host of the little flower angels. They are here right now. They love your flowers, and they dearly love you. They are fighting over which flower they get to take care of. The Lord has sent them in response to your prayers, and they are here to help care for each rose and flower. He has sent along are more little flower angels than you have flowers, and they all want to help you."

With that, she flung her head back, threw up her hands up in the air, and laughed such a hearty laugh that it shook her whole body. She went on to exclaim that each little angel had on bright colored mud boots. Flower, fountain, and waterway angels are real. They are small and delicate with a fairy-like appearance. Flower angels have sparkling gowns, much like the well-known Tinkerbell. They love to serve the Lord by tending to His gardens, fountains, and waterways in heaven but closer even here on earth.

My heart immediately filled up with great joy, and I felt the overflow of God's love and goodness right then and there. I went on to tell my dear friend that I had actually been praying for quite some time that the Lord would please send His small flower and waterway angels to care for my flowers each night.

    I had set out several solar lights so these delightful angels would feel more at home while they work hard here in my yard— and yours too if you should ask the Lord. Heaven has so much light, and I understand that they too love the light, and are naturally drawn to it. Such a happy thing!

    So, in reality, the Lord allowed me to understand that He, indeed, had answered my prayers, as I had asked Him to send the angels to help me care for the flowers. He loves all of His beautiful creation, including our yards and His delicate angels.

    With that, whoosh! My dear friend threw her SUV in reverse and drove out the driveway waving and smiling with delight as she went. I sensed a great deal of joy bubbles and gladness that the Lord had just released through her insight to me. These adorable angels with boots had been spotted in my rose garden by others as well. This was not the first time these colorful heavenly creatures had been sighted in my rose garden. It is not uncommon at all for people to see, smell, or even hear the little angels, or also the huge warring angels, as they walk by on the sidewalk, or come for a visit.

    To this day, I look out for these fair, delicate heavenly visitors in my little rose garden…and I am so blessed to see, hear, and sense their presence often.

    Now my top-secret, flower-power weapon is out! Praying for, believing for, and anticipating heaven's help for my lovely flowers.

PRAYER

Talking from my heart to God's loving heart is one of my top-secret special ways to connect with heaven. It is in our Father's heart I find real answers, comfort, and hope for my own soul. It is in Elohim's heart that we can find rich and abundant beauty, along with fragrance and joy in our roses and flowers.

I specifically pray and ask Father God to please bless my plants with His loving touch. With genuine faith, I also ask Him to send His flower and waterway angels to help the flowers flourish. Together, flowers and angels, big and small all sing, dance, and clap their hands in praise and worship of the King of kings, and Lord of lords.

Let the rivers clap their hands;
Let the hills be joyful together before the Lord

— PSALMS 98:8-9A

Honestly, I simply believe, with all my heart, that God does bless my flowers and home. Know that He wants to bless you, your home, and flowers as well. I urge you; dear fellow rose lover, go ahead and pray that the Creator of the universe will bless your plants and flowers too. You may be delighted and surprised at what He will do or whom He may send to bless you!

Shout joyfully to the Lord, all the earth;
Break forth in song, rejoice, and sing praises.

— PSALMS 98:4

ROSE BUDS OF BLESSINGS

- Beautiful roses work hard to make you happy with lots of beautiful blooms, so be sure to feed them plenty of good organic food.

- Your rose babies will wake up quicker and grow stronger if they are tucked in warm winter blankets.

- Surprisingly, roses aren't vegetarians as they like a little fish meat and blood meal in their snacks.

- Keep your roses' feet clean, and you will have less fussing with bad bugs and disease.

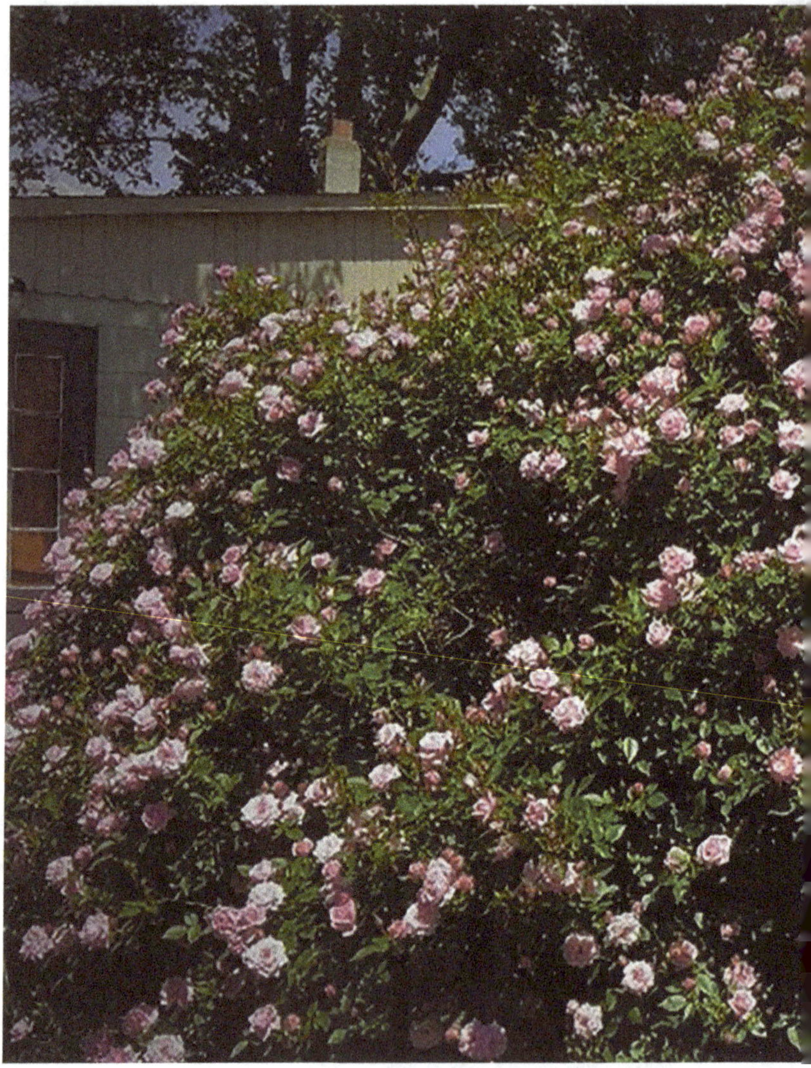

This humongous, extremely vigorous, hardy, and disease resistant miniature rose, Jeanne Lajoie, does my heart wonders. Look at the sheer volume of cheery powder-puff-pink roses that envelop this glorious 8 - 9 foot fountain bush, just out my back door. Thank You, dear Father God, for Your lovely bouquet, from Your loving hands to my grateful heart. Bless You, Abba!

This is not

THE END

No, beloved reader.

This is only the beginning of a whole new chapter in your beautiful and much-loved, gardening life, as your walk with The Master Gardener in the garden of life.

May you grow in faith, hope, and love, walking with "The Rose," your beautiful, fragrant, and loving Abba, Father God.

THE END NOTES FOR A NEW BEGINNING

I am the rose of Sharon,
And the lily of the valleys.

— SONG OF SOLOMON 2:1

Dear Friend,

You know and love the beautiful rose, but do you know and love the rose's loving and beautiful Creator God? Do you know the Lover of your soul, Jesus Christ the KING of kings and LORD of lords? He and His Heavenly Father and precious Holy Spirit, all love you more than you can possibly know. They want you to be sure that you will live with them forever and ever in heaven. They lovingly want you to receive the free gift of eternal life, light, and love that only they can offer to you.

Does darkness surround you? Are you afraid of the future? Are you anxious and feeling unloved? Have you lost your peace and hope? You do not have to walk in darkness one more minute! There is hope and peace and real freedom in accepting and walking in the light of Jesus.

The horrible price of sin was paid for by the blood of Jesus Christ, as Lord and Savior of the entire world— every tribe, every nation, and every color and race. This priceless gift is available right now. It is free and simple to us. We just have to receive it by faith. Just believe in your heart that God loves you. He hears and forgives you by His grace. Receive Jesus's blood and salvation. He is the only One Who can save you for a life in heaven. Heaven and hell are both real and both go on forever.

Receive eternal life today. Simply pray this prayer out loud and believe in your heart:

Dear Jesus,

I confess that I am a sinner.
I believe that You are the Son of God,
And that You shed Your precious blood
On the cross for me and all my sins.

Please forgive me for my sins.
Cleanse my heart from all unrighteousness.
I thank You, Jesus, for saving me now.
I receive this new and blessed life by faith.

Thank you for the new life that I now have in Jesus Christ. Amen.

> *If you confess with your mouth the Lord Jesus and*
> *believe in your heart*
> *That God has raised Him from the dead,*
> *You will be saved.*
> *For with the heart one believes unto righteousness,*
> *And with the mouth confession is made unto salvation.*
>
> — ROMANS 10:9–10

If you have just prayed this prayer, please let me know. I would love to encourage you in your newfound faith and family. Write me today at: heavenslovelight@gmail.com or spettitgallery@gmail.com

*May God bless you
with His eternal life,
love, joy, peace, hope, and comfort,
today and always,
in Jesus's All-Powerful name, amen.*

I look forward to seeing you in heaven— forever. Please do come visit me in my eternal rose garden where we shall sit, laugh, and have beautiful cookies with our glorious cups of perfect tea. Our beloved Father God will come visit us in the garden as well.

RESOURCES

ART & WEBSITES BY SUSAN

www.SPettitGallery.com
www.heavenslovelight.com

ENTREPRENEUR HELP

Small Business Development Center – No-cost consultation for your small business in your state - https://americassbdc.org/

SUSAN'S ART, BOOKS & GIFTS

Amazon.com - www.amazon.com

...and BOOKS TOO! - www.andbookstooonline.com

Barnes & Noble - https://www.barnesandnoble.com/

Heaven's Love Light - www.heavenslovelight.com

S. Pettit Gallery – Custom artwork or readymade art & gift items, please feel free to contact me and ask if there is a special piece you want created - www.spettitgallery.com

The Diamond Shop - www.thediamondshop.com

OWN-ROOT ROSES

Heirloom Garden Roses - www.heirloomroses.com

Northland Rosarium - www.northlandrosarium.com

RECOMMENDED READING

Gladstar, Rosemary. *Rosemary Gladstar's Herbal Recipes for Vibrant Health.* Massachusetts: Storey Publishing, 2001, 2008.

Green, Douglas. *Tender Roses for Tough Climates.* Vermont: Chapters Publishing, LTD., 1997.

Oster, Maggie. *The Rose Book*. Pennsylvania: Rodale Press, 1994.

Pettit, Susan. *Color My World, A 31-Day Devotional, Prayer and Coloring Jou*rnal. Florida: Xulon Press, 2017.

Reddell, Rayford Clayton. *A Year in the Life a Rose, A Guide to Growing Roses from Coast to Coast.* New York: Harmony Books, 1996.

Shaudys, Phyllis V. *Herbal Treasures, Inspiring Month-by-Month Projects For Gardening, Cooking and Crafts.* Vermont: Storey Communications, Inc., 1990.

Vermeulen, Nico. *The Complete Rose Encyclopedia, A Guide to the Selection, Care and Beauty of Roses for Your Garden.* New York: Gramercy Books, 1998.

Walheim, Lance. *The Natural Rose Gardener.* Arizona: Ironwood Press, 1994.

ROSES

David Austin English Roses
https://www.davidaustinroses.com/

Heirloom Garden Roses
www.heirloomroses.com

Northland Rosarium
www.northlandrosarium.com

Patt's Garden Center
www.pattsgardencenter.com

SUPPLIES

Felco Pruning Shears (F 32) - High Performance Swiss-Made One-Hand Garden Pruners, high quality, and will last a lifetime if maintained.
https://www.felco.com/

Garden Shears – I like small hand-held trimmers.

Soil amendments: SUPERthrive, dried kelp, blood meal, azomite, mycorrhizae – Local hardware and garden shops

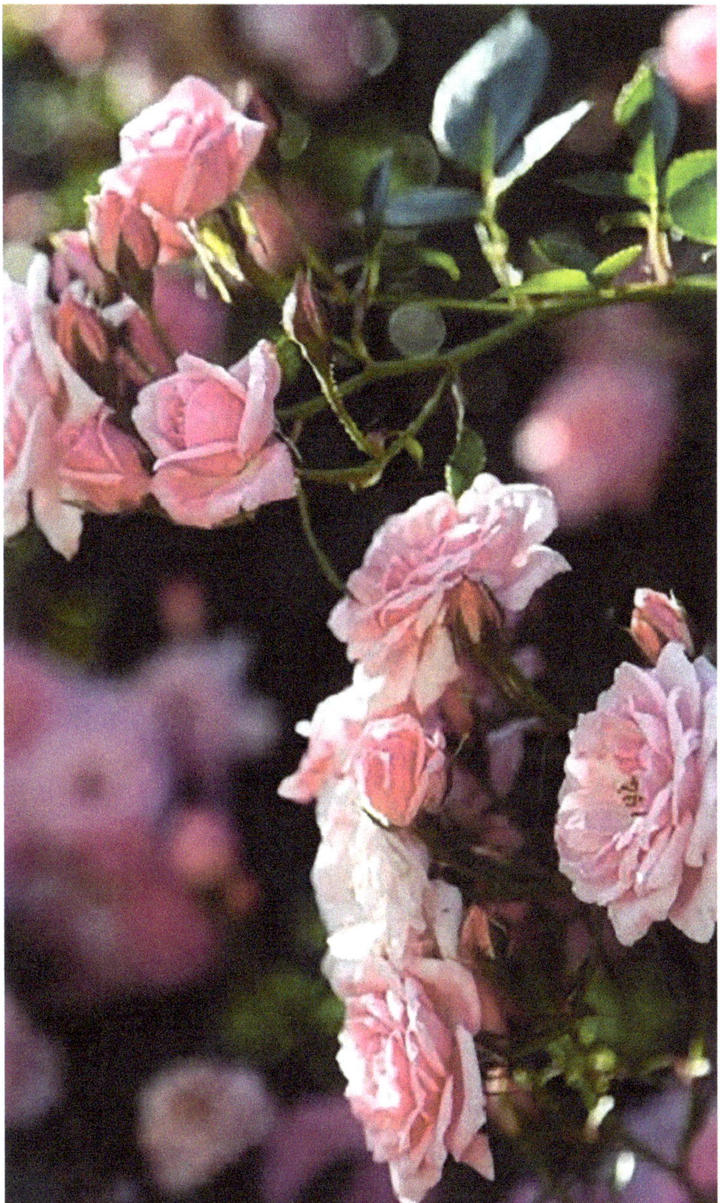

ABOUT THE AUTHOR AND ARTIST

Susan Pettit has loved roses and flowers from her earliest childhood memories. At the age of five, she knew that she would grow up to be an artist; so, she would stay in from recess to begin "practicing" for that dream ahead. After she received her BA degree in Commercial Art from Pensacola Christian College, she went on to teach college art classes, work as an illustrator, and graphic designer.

She works in her home studio and gallery, S. Pettit Gallery. She is working on writing and illustrated books, creating many commissioned fine art pieces, and painting guardian angels and prophetic art pieces as well. She gathers inspiration from the Creator's handiwork in her rose and flower gardens.

The Lord gave her a desire through the Father's heart of love and light to help bring heaven to earth around the world through her art and books. It is a great joy to share her flowers and a cup of tea with guests who are seeking prayer or a word of encouragement while working with angels and the supernatural armies of heaven.

She considers some of her biggest blessings to be her three beautiful grown daughters and creative young grandson.

Her next big heavenly assignment is writing and illustrating several mini-series of children's books. The first book set for the little people will be on questions on heavenly mysteries.

See more of Susan's artwork and projects or purchase more copies of her books at:

www.SPettitGallery.com
www.heavenslovelight.com

You can also purchase her books at:

www.amazon.com
www.barnesandnoble.com/
www.andbookstooonline.com
www.thediamondshop.com
www.trilogy.tv/bookstore

Susan would love to hear from you. You can email your comments, questions, or ask for more information about commissioned art or the upcoming children's books at:

SPettitGallery@gmail.com
heavenslovelight@gmail.com

f Follow, Like and Share on Facebook, Instagram, and LinkedIn

*Look for my next books in
the Rose Trilogy coming soon!*

ENJOY ROSES EVERY DAY

Volume 2

How to Romance "The Rose" Inside

Learn how to bring those blooming roses inside with beauty, loving hospitality, and creative gifts, as I share many of my secrets and family favorite recipes.

❀

ENJOY ROSES EVERY DAY

Volume 3

How to Romance "The Rose" Heartside

Learn how to fall more in love with King Jesus, The One True Rose, and how to see into the supernatural and work with the Angelic Host in your life every day.

CHILDREN'S BOOKS

coming soon

WHERE IN THE WORLD IS HEAVEN?

On her art desk now, Susan is writing and illustrating a children's book based on the true story of little Jake and how he missed his dear grandma after she died and went to heaven. He gets out the big World Atlas to find her new home. You and the kids will be delighted and surprised where he finds heaven and her new address.

Check Susan's website for updates and details on the five books in the upcoming *Where and Who* series for little ones: *Where in the World Is Heaven? Where in the World Did I Come From? Who in the World Is God? Who in the World Is Jesus?* and *Who in the World Is Holy Spirit?*

Please visit Susan Pettit's art gallery for books and more art at:

www.SPettitGallery.com
www.heavenslovelight.com

COLOR MY WORLD

This warm and grace-filled 31-Day Devotional, Prayer, and Coloring Journal of light, love, and hope is filled with encouragement. Susan shares from her treasure chest jewels of hope and encouragement that the Lord gave her in the blackest hours. These word pictures share how the Creator showed His Love Light and colored her dark world with the brilliant light of courage and inspiration and now for you as well. You can read or journal inside and/or color as well.

Color My World, (Soft Cover ISBN 978-1-5456-0069-6) is available for purchase at:

www. SPettitGallery.com
www.Amazon.com
Barnes & Noble bookstore
...and BOOKS Too!

CPSIA information can be obtained
at www.ICGtesting.com
Printed in the USA
BVHW091541290922
648202BV00002B/2